Number 128
Winter 2010

New Directions for Evaluation

Sandra Mathison
Editor-in-Chief

Evaluating Strategy

Patricia A. Patrizi
Michael Quinn Patton
Editors

EVALUATING STRATEGY
Patricia A. Patrizi, Michael Quinn Patton (eds.)
New Directions for Evaluation, no. 128
Sandra Mathison, Editor-in-Chief

Microfilm copies of issues and articles are available in 16mm and 35mm, as well as microfiche in 105mm, through University Microfilms Inc., 300 North Zeeb Road, Ann Arbor, MI 48106-1346.

New Directions for Evaluation is indexed in Cambridge Scientific Abstracts (CSA/CIG), Contents Pages in Education (T & F), Higher Education Abstracts (Claremont Graduate University), Social Services Abstracts (CSA/CIG), Sociological Abstracts (CSA/CIG), and Worldwide Political Sciences Abstracts (CSA/CIG).

NEW DIRECTIONS FOR EVALUATION (ISSN 1097-6736, electronic ISSN 1534-875X) is part of The Jossey-Bass Education Series and is published quarterly by Wiley Subscription Services, Inc., A Wiley Company, at Jossey-Bass, 989 Market Street, San Francisco, CA 94103-1741.

SUBSCRIPTIONS cost $89 for U.S./Canada/Mexico; $113 international. For institutions, agencies, and libraries, $271 U.S.; $311 Canada/Mexico; $345 international. Prices subject to change.

EDITORIAL CORRESPONDENCE should be addressed to the Editor-in-Chief, Sandra Mathison, University of British Columbia, 2125 Main Mall, Vancouver, BC V6T 1Z4, Canada.

www.josseybass.com

Editorial Policy and Procedures

New Directions for Evaluation, a quarterly sourcebook, is an official publication of the American Evaluation Association. The journal publishes empirical, methodological, and theoretical works on all aspects of evaluation. A reflective approach to evaluation is an essential strand to be woven through every issue. The editors encourage issues that have one of three foci: (1) craft issues that present approaches, methods, or techniques that can be applied in evaluation practice, such as the use of templates, case studies, or survey research; (2) professional issues that present topics of import for the field of evaluation, such as utilization of evaluation or locus of evaluation capacity; (3) societal issues that draw out the implications of intellectual, social, or cultural developments for the field of evaluation, such as the women's movement, communitarianism, or multiculturalism. A wide range of substantive domains is appropriate for *New Directions for Evaluation;* however, the domains must be of interest to a large audience within the field of evaluation. We encourage a diversity of perspectives and experiences within each issue, as well as creative bridges between evaluation and other sectors of our collective lives.

The editors do not consider or publish unsolicited single manuscripts. Each issue of the journal is devoted to a single topic, with contributions solicited, organized, reviewed, and edited by a guest editor. Issues may take any of several forms, such as a series of related chapters, a debate, or a long article followed by brief critical commentaries. In all cases, the proposals must follow a specific format, which can be obtained from the editor-in-chief. These proposals are sent to members of the editorial board and to relevant substantive experts for peer review. The process may result in acceptance, a recommendation to revise and resubmit, or rejection. However, the editors are committed to working constructively with potential guest editors to help them develop acceptable proposals.

Sandra Mathison, Editor-in-Chief
University of British Columbia
2125 Main Mall
Vancouver, BC V6T 1Z4
CANADA
e-mail: nde@eval.org

CONTENTS

Editors' Notes

This issue of *New Directions for Evaluation* focuses on evaluating strategy. Strategy is a new unit of analysis for evaluation, because traditionally, evaluation has focused on projects, programs, products, policies, and personnel. Organizational development makes the organization the unit of analysis for assessing organizational effectiveness, usually focused on mission fulfillment. So what does it mean to treat *strategy* as the evaluation focus, as the thing evaluated? Inquiry into that question is what the contributors to this issue have undertaken together.

We have been working together for more than a decade on the Evaluation Roundtable, a network of major philanthropic foundation evaluators coming together periodically as a community of practice to engage around common concerns. In planning each Roundtable, Patricia A. Patrizi, the Roundtable's founder and convener, and co-editor of this issue, polls network participants and philanthropic leaders about their priority concerns and gathers data about current evaluation practices and uses. Previous Roundtables had focused on evaluating large-scale initiatives, evaluating organizational mission, building relationships between program staff and evaluators, and evaluating under conditions of complexity (Patton, 2010). In 2008, the consultative process led to a focus on *evaluating strategy*. Senior foundation program staff and evaluators reported that their chief executive officers and boards were increasingly focused on overall foundation strategy rather than specific programs, and they were demanding strategic evaluation.

In preparing for that meeting we found no evaluation literature that directly addressed evaluating strategy. But once strategy had emerged as the focus, we noticed an emphasis on strategy wherever we looked, in government initiatives, not-for-profit conferences, international collaborations, and, especially, private-sector leadership and management. It was a bit like a couple having their first child and suddenly, everywhere you look, you see pregnant women. Everywhere we looked, we saw a concern with being strategic: thinking strategically, acting strategically, and being strategic, all of which led quite directly to evaluating strategically. That gave birth to this issue.

The first chapter provides an overview of what it means to evaluate strategy. What is strategy? How is strategy different from a theory of change or logic model? What are the implications of treating strategy as an evaluand? We review how strategy is viewed in various sectors with consideration of the evaluation implications of those perspectives. We conclude by offering a framework for making distinctions about different kinds of strategy based on the work of management scholar Henry Mintzberg that focuses on *Tracking Strategies* (Mintzberg, 2007). Mintzberg was the expert presenter at

NEW DIRECTIONS FOR EVALUATION, no. 128, Winter 2010 © Wiley Periodicals, Inc., and the American Evaluation Association.   Published online in Wiley Online Library (wileyonlinelibrary.com) • DOI: 10.1002/ev.342

the 2008 Evaluation Roundtable convening at the Robert Wood Johnson Foundation that focused on *evaluating strategy* and inspired this issue.

Chapters 2, 3, and 4 are case examples of evaluating strategy. Chapter 2 presents the experiences of the International Development Research Centre (IDRC) in undertaking evaluation of strategy to inform their strategic planning. IDRC is a Crown Corporation created by the Parliament of Canada in 1970 to help developing countries use science and technology to find practical, long-term solutions to the social, economic, and environmental problems they face. IDRC works in close collaboration with researchers from the developing world in their search for the means to build healthier, more equitable, and more prosperous societies. IDRC has become a leader in international development evaluation with worldwide training in the Outcome Mapping approach it pioneered and participation in international evaluation forums and networks. In 2009, IDRC's Evaluation Unit commissioned an external review of the Centre's corporate strategy. The review identified tensions between IDRC's strategic perspective and its strategic position that had implications for how priorities are set and decisions made within the Centre's programs. The lessons they learned and uses they made of strategy-focused evaluation affirms this as an important new direction for evaluation.

Chapter 3 presents an evaluation of some 20 years of strategic work on end-of-life initiatives undertaken by the Robert Wood Johnson Foundation (RWJF). The chapter title foreshadows the evaluation's important lesson: *Death is certain. Strategy isn't.* The Foundation commissioned Patrizi Associates, led by co-editor Patricia A. Patrizi, to conduct a strategic assessment of its investments in "improving the end of life." The purpose of the assessment was to create an overall learning opportunity for Foundation staff and others interested in how foundations construct and execute grant-making strategies. The evaluation sought to document strategy and field-level effects related to the portfolio as a whole, effects not always noticeable when individual programs, projects, and grants are evaluated. The fact that the review covers a period of 20 years is, in and of itself, unusual in evaluation. The case illustrates and illuminates *evaluating strategy* by looking across and synthesizing two decades of discrete projects, programs, and grants *with particular attention to a few critical strategic decisions.* Strategy decisions involve forks in the road: Do we go that way or this way? This case involved some clear strategic alternatives and the subsequent decisions—their implications, consequences, and results—are evaluable and, in this example, evaluated. Strategy became the thread that runs through those 20 years of work and provides focus for a very complex set of interventions and cumulative evaluation of multifaceted and diverse initiatives. The evaluation concludes that key knowledgeables credit the Foundation with "building the field" of end-of-life care in the United States. The evaluation presents the evidence for this conclusion and analyzes what this means. Seven key factors that contributed to field building are examined and a strategic model is generated. Implications for foundation strategy and evaluating strategy are discussed.

Chapter 4 is a retrospective case study of the devolution strategy of the U.S. federal government beginning in the mid-1990s. At that time, the U.S. government embarked on a policy called "devolution"—shifting powers, responsibilities, and funding from the federal level of government to the state level, and sometimes the local level, for a number of social welfare programs, beginning with the cash assistance program for low-income families formerly known as Aid to Families with Dependent Children (AFDC), commonly called "welfare." The embarkation event, a law called the Personal Responsibility and Work Opportunities Reauthorization Act (PRWORA), was radical—overturning a social safety net that had been built over several decades. And it was politically divisive because the shift of authority away from the federal government was accompanied by a shift from an open-ended system of income assistance to budget limits, time limits for receiving cash assistance, and requirements for cash assistance recipients to work. Advocates for low-income families worried that some would be left destitute and their children consigned to foster care; public-policy analysts worried that states, now freer to set welfare policies, would begin "a race to the bottom" to reduce benefits and assistance to low-income families; the authors of the PRWORA legislation worried that Congressional intent would be undermined by liberals in government and in nonprofit entities seeking to "soften" the provisions of the law. The W. K. Kellogg Foundation decided to support a major multistakeholder initiative to evaluate the processes and effects of federal devolution, including building the capacity of community-based organizations and state-based researchers to participate in the evaluation. The result was the Devolution Initiative, a 7-year, $56 million project with 31 grantees that was, itself, evaluated through a $6.3 million evaluation. The case study of that evaluation was originally written as an evaluation teaching case for the Evaluation Roundtable. Three such evaluation teaching cases were published in an earlier *New Directions for Evaluation* (Patrizi & Patton, 2005). The Devolution Initiative case has not been previously published.

As we planned this issue, we thought it would be instructive to revisit the Devolution Initiative story told here through the lens of strategy to illuminate issues of evaluating strategy at the different levels and in the varying but interrelated arenas involved in the case.

The final chapter, Chapter 5, looks at methodological issues that arise in evaluating strategy. The three case studies in this issue (Chapters 2–4) are retrospective case studies, looking back to elucidate, track, and evaluate strategy. The methods chapter presents the methodological challenges addressed and the lessons Patrizi and her colleagues learned in conducting the retrospective strategic evaluation of end-of-life initiatives featured in the third chapter. In addition, the chapter examines how strategy can be evaluated prospectively and the implications of a prospective and proactive approach to evaluating strategy.

As readers engage with the case studies and overview chapters on theory (Chapter 1) and methods (Chapter 5), we invite you to join our inquiry: What does it mean to evaluate *strategy*? What are the consequences of treating *strategy* as the unit of analysis, the evaluand, the focus of evaluation? What are the implications of this new direction for evaluation theory, methods, practice, and, ultimately, use? This issue is merely the beginning of inquiry into these questions.

References

Mintzberg, H. (2007). *Tracking strategies*. New York: Oxford University Press.
Patrizi, P., & Patton, M. Q. (Eds.). (2005). *Teaching evaluation using the case method. New Directions for Evaluation, 105.*
Patton, M. Q. (2010). *Developmental evaluation: Applying complexity concepts to enhance innovation and use.* New York: Guilford.

Patricia A. Patrizi
Michael Quinn Patton
Editors

PATRICIA A. PATRIZI *is chair of the Evaluation Roundtable and principal of Patrizi Associates, Philadelphia.*

MICHAEL QUINN PATTON *is founder and director of Utilization-Focused Evaluation, and author of the book by that name. He is a former president of the American Evaluation Association.*

1

Strategy as the Focus for Evaluation

Michael Quinn Patton, Patricia A. Patrizi

Abstract

*Strategic thinking and planning have long been the focus of management train-
ing and organizational development, but strategy is a new unit of analysis for
evaluation. The authors examine the increasing attention given to being strategic in the private sector, in government, in philanthropy, and in the not-for-profit
sectors. To respond and adapt to concerns about the implementation and impacts
of strategy, strategy needs to be evaluated. The authors look at what strategy is,
offer a framework for evaluating strategy, consider issues in strategic evaluation,
and examine opportunities for strategic learning based on evaluating strategy.*
© Wiley Periodicals, Inc., and the American Evaluation Association.

Thinking and Evaluating Strategically

Unless a variety of opinions are laid before us,
we have no opportunity of selection, but are bound
of necessity to adopt the particular view which may
have been brought forward
      Herodotus, Greek historian, 5th century B.C.

The contemporary word *strategy* derives from the ancient Greek word *strategos,* which meant to think like a general. The term originated, then, as a reference to military strategy, but in ancient Greece military leaders were often also territorial governors. *Strategoi,* then, were politicians as well as generals.

Strategy is a new unit of analysis for evaluation. The *Encyclopedia of Evaluation* (Mathison, 2005) has an entry on "strategic planning" but nothing on strategy as an evaluand or on evaluating strategy. Traditionally, evaluation has focused on projects and programs. Organizational development makes the organization the unit of analysis for assessing organizational effectiveness, usually focused on mission fulfillment. Management, in contrast, often focuses on *strategy* as the defining determinant of effectiveness. The language of strategy permeates senior management initiatives in government, philanthropy, the private sector, and the not-for-profit world. Being sensitive and responsive to primary intended users of evaluation has become a hallmark of effective and useful practice. In that sense, being sensitive and responsive to the language and concepts used by primary intended users is a *strategy* for enhancing the relevance and utility of evaluations. We came to focus on the question of what it means to evaluate strategy, because we observed that our senior management clients in all sectors were talking *not* about theories of change or logic models, but about being strategic: Strategic thinking. Strategic planning. Strategic results. Being strategic. Strategy execution. Adapting strategically. And, yes, *evaluating* strategy. In this regard, we are working in the tradition of that eminent evaluation pioneer, Sir Winston Churchill (1874–1965), who is reputed to have observed: "However beautiful the strategy, you should occasionally look at the results."

One of the reasons we think that evaluators have been slow to focus on evaluating strategy is that strategy is closely associated with planning, strategic planning, and as evaluators we don't do planning, we do evaluation. But what's been happening in the world of management is a movement away from a focus on strategy as equivalent to planning, something we'll have more to say about later. For now, we want to emphasize that evaluating strategy is not about evaluating strategic planning, or even strategic plans. It's about evaluating *strategy* itself. And that, we shall argue, makes all the difference.

We begin, then, with a brief overview of how the language of strategy has come to permeate management thinking and writings about organizational effectiveness. We'll then examine some of the diverse definitions of strategy and what it means to be strategic. Then we'll review what we consider to be a particularly useful framework for evaluating strategy. Finally, we'll consider the implications for evaluation of treating strategy as a distinct *evaluand,* that is, a specific unit of analysis and target for evaluation.

Strategy as a Focus

We want to begin with the larger context by giving some sense of how strategy is talked about by organizational leaders, board members, academics, management consultants, best-selling authors of management books, and influential professional development trainers. As an interdisciplinary and transdisciplinary field, it is important for evaluation to keep abreast of developments in the larger world. What are leaders talking about? How do they conceptualize the challenges they face and the value-added they bring to their organizations? What do they worry about? What are they seeking to improve? *That which concerns them should concern us.* At least that's the premise under which we're working.

Strategic management has long been a private-sector focus and there are lots of books about *strategic management* (e.g., David, 2008; Hill & Jones, 2009; Hitt, Ireland, & Hoskisson, 2010; Pearce & Robinson, 2010). You'll also find a plethora of books on related themes like strategic thinking (Haines, 2007; Sloan, 2006) and strategic planning, including books targeted to the government and not-for-profit sectors (e.g., Bryson, 2004; La Piana, 2008). But we found nothing on *strategic evaluation.*

There is, however, a recognized field of strategy consulting. This is one of the specializations monitored in the annual management consulting recruitment channel report. The 2010 report found that strategy consulting is especially vulnerable to economic conditions.

> Strategy consulting, often the quickest to be hit in a downturn, can also be amongst the last to recover during an upturn. In many respects it's the most discretionary type of consulting spend there is—and this has spillover effects on the hiring trends within strategy consulting. Given this, it is therefore heartening for the industry as a whole to see a general consensus that strategy consulting hiring will gather pace this year—one of the strongest indicators that as an industry we perceive the worst to be very much behind us. (TopConsultant, 2010, p. 10)

One approach to strategy consulting is *strategic performance management.* For example, Rick Johnson, a private-sector management consultant who founded CEO Strategist LLC, markets himself as a "leadership strategist" and asserts that: "Success during the most significant economic challenge since the depression, is Strategic Performance Management" (Johnson, 2008, p. 1). He argues that the big mistake of the past has been too much focus on performance measurement rather than on *strategic* performance management, which he presents as a "platform for the effective management of individuals and teams in order to achieve high levels of organizational success . . . Strategic performance management is a holistic process, bringing together many of the elements which go to make up the successful practice of people management, including in particular—learning and development" (p. 1). A related approach, Strategy-Driven Execution Management, is a proprietary model based on monitoring the implementation and outcomes of strategy (Keyne Insight, 2010).

Government initiatives also use the language of strategy. For example, the federal Office of Management and Budget created a task force "E-Government

Strategy: Simplified Delivery of Services to Citizens" (Office of Management and Budget, 2002) and the Congressional Research Service (2007) reviewed "State E-Government Strategies" to identify "best practices and applications." A widely read Harvard Business School casebook on The Strategy-Focused Government Organization equates being strategy focused and evaluating strategy with use of the balanced scorecard (Kaplan & Norton, 2000). The news is filled with debates about government policy and reform strategies in education, health, the environment, and new directions for foreign-policy strategies, global climate management strategies, and economic-development strategies. As in private-sector management and government policy debates, admonitions to think strategically have permeated the philanthropic sector.

Strategic Philanthropy

Word Spy, a Web site that tracks new words and phrases, credits the earliest usage of "strategic philanthropy" to Ruth Walker commenting on "business philanthropy seen as an investment" in a 1983 article in the *Christian Science Monitor.* Strategic philanthropy "sounds like a contradiction in terms. But observers in the field of corporate social responsibility—which includes philanthropy, volunteerism, and 'social investment'—are arguing that corporate America gives most effectively when it gives to serve enlightened self-interest" (Walker, 1983).

Since that time the phrase has become widely used and has a variety of different meanings and usages. An International Network on Strategic Philanthropy has emerged that associates the phrase with a number of dimensions related to effectiveness:

> Strategic philanthropy refers both to the working philosophy and the program strategies of a foundation. It originates from an entrepreneurial view of foundation activities, which focuses around strategy, key competencies and striving for effective contributions to social change. Strategic philanthropy . . . involves institutions that are driven by:
>
> a vision of the desirable society of the future,
>
> a distinct value orientation in their activities,
>
> a concept of social change to the effect of greater social justice rather than the mere grant-making to address social problems,
>
> the conviction that foundations serve as laboratories to develop model solutions, new ways of thinking, and new understanding for resolving societal problems,
>
> the awareness that innovative models and approaches should include both blueprints and a focus on practical implementation and applicability,

a concern for the effectiveness of their philanthropic endeavors,

a proactive approach, be it in their own activities, be it in partnering or grant-making,

an awareness for capacity building and organizational learning among grantees/partners,

a public policy orientation driven by the potential of taking project results to scale on policy levels,

the insight that philanthropy provides for investment in the production of public goods, preferably aiming at innovations or increased effectiveness. (International Network on Strategic Philanthropy, 2005; Putnam, 2010)

Paul Brest is president of the William and Flora Hewlett Foundation, former Dean of Stanford Law School, and coauthor of the book *Money Well Spent: A Strategic Plan for Smart Philanthropy* (Brest & Harvey, 2008). He argues that "[T]he fundamental tenets of strategic philanthropy are that funders and their grantees should have clear goals, strategies based on sound theories of change, and robust methods for assessing progress toward their goals (Brest, 2010, p. 47), criteria that should resonate with evaluators. But according to a recent report from the Center for Effective Philanthropy (2009), although most foundation executives believe it is important to have an explicit strategy to manage and inform their grant-making decisions, relatively few foundations have actually developed one (Buteau, Buchanan, & Brock, 2009).

The philanthropic Evaluation Roundtable is a network of major philanthropic foundation evaluators. This group meets periodically to consider cutting-edge issues in evaluation. The May 2008 gathering at the Robert Wood Johnson Foundation focused on evaluating strategy. Prior to the meeting, telephone interviews were conducted with senior staff from 14 of the largest philanthropic foundations in the United States focusing on identifying patterns of strategy development, use, and evaluation. Two-thirds of the foundations reported that they had gone through a major change in strategy in the past 18 months, often stimulated by a change in leadership. Strategy articulation was most often associated with strategic planning, but respondents reported that little attention was paid to evaluating strategy. They also reported some push back against the pervasive attention to strategy: "I am strategied out"; "The process [of strategic planning] is becoming a monster."

Foundations devote substantial time, resources, and staff to concerns about strategy, and the language of "being strategic" permeates their organizational cultures and leadership rhetoric, but the findings identified a number of perceived weaknesses in how large and prestigious philanthropic foundations approach strategy formulation—*and a general absence of strategy evaluation.* Moreover, little is invested in ongoing learning about strategy as it evolves. The broad participation in the Evaluation Roundtable by the leaders in philanthropic evaluation and their enthusiastic reaction to the deliberations about evaluating strategy during the Roundtable conference suggests that this is an important emerging direction with implications for evaluation generally.

Ricardo Millett, former Director of Evaluation for the W. K. Kellogg Foundation and a pioneer in philanthropic evaluation, recently reflected on the state of foundation evaluation in presenting the 2010 Mary E. Corcoran keynote address at the Minnesota Evaluation Studies Institute Annual Conference. He emphasized the absence of strategic evaluation.

> We are still in the infancy stage of evaluation diffusion in the foundation community. I would venture that seventy-five percent or more of all foundations do not apply evaluation tools in their grant making decisions and programming processes, and if they do it is primarily focused on the grantees' performance. Few see "results/outcomes/impact" as a function of their efforts in relation to grantees' efforts informed and framed by some level of *strategic intentionality.*
>
> So what is wrong with this picture? Why do the majority of foundations, while perhaps convinced that having a strategy is important to effective "social betterment" achievement, not engage us more? Is it because our methods are too obtuse and esoteric? Or that we are too expensive and slow in delivering useful information for management decisions. Whatever the reason, I believe that the onus is on us to figure out what is going on and fix it. We need to be more proactive if we want to lead. We need to figure out why the great majority of foundations and non-profits are not understanding or applying our tools. We need to lead the discussion about why the application of our tools can be useful. (Millett, 2010)

Millett went on to recommend that evaluators form a "strategic philanthropy technical assistance team" to learn and work with interested foundations and a group of their grantees to translate their current mission statements to a more explicit strategy that could inform grant decisions and management—and be strategically evaluated. The proposed technical assistance would focus on strategy specification and evaluation. He concluded:

> We must find the inspiration to meet foundations where they are. We must find ways to translate evaluation logic and methods into easier to understand and usable modules, facilitate focus on mission, clear strategies and measurable indicators related to goals and strategy. (Millett, 2010)

Millett's observations about the absence of strategic evaluation were informed by research from the Center for Effective Philanthropy on *Essentials of Foundation Strategy* (Buteau et al., 2009). The study analyzed how nearly 200 foundation executives and program officers made decisions. They categorized and compared more strategic with less strategic grant makers. They found that more strategic grant makers were:

Able to explain in depth the logic that undergirded their work and the connections between what they did and what they sought to achieve
More likely to seek external feedback
More transparent in communicating their strategies
More engaged in evaluation

In disseminating their findings, the researchers have emphasized thinking strategically about philanthropic work, especially in deciding what new initiatives and approaches to undertake. Whether new ways of doing things make any sense for a particular foundation depends. Depends on what? "It's all about strategy—and strategy, by definition, is not one size fits all" (Buchanan & Buteau, 2010, p. 32).

This emphasis on thinking strategically and evaluating strategy mirrors the views of participants in the philanthropic Evaluation Roundtable. So, with all this attention to strategy in all sectors of engagement—private sector, government, not-for-profit programs, and philanthropy—what is it?

What Is Strategy?

Perception is strong and sight weak. In strategy it is
important to see distant things as if they were close
and to take a distanced view of close things
      Miyamoto Musashi (1584–1645), legendary Japanese swordsman

Strategy is generally understood to be about where an organization is headed and how it intends to get there. Strategies can be visionary or concrete, very long-term or relatively short-term (say 3 years), explicit or implicit, meaningful or mere window-dressing, and agreed on or a source of conflict. These are but a few of the dimensions along which strategies vary and which, by the way, can become criteria for evaluating strategy. The great variety of approaches to strategy and strategic management led strategic management scholars Mintzberg, Lampel, and Ahlstrand (2005) to call their review: *Strategy Safari: The Complete Guide Through the Wilds of Strategic Management*. So, the first question that arises in evaluating strategy is this: What do the people using the word *strategy* mean by it? A related question is: How important to the organization's leadership and culture is thinking strategically, or being strategic, or being perceived as being strategic? Where attention to strategy and strategic thinking are highly valued, opportunities to evaluate strategy will exist.

NEW DIRECTIONS FOR EVALUATION • DOI: 10.1002/ev

In looking at various frameworks that might inform evaluating strategy, we resonate to a behavioral approach in which strategy is evaluated by examining patterns of behavior—what the organization actually does—not just its rhetoric about strategy and strategic plans. Herbert Simon, one of the preeminent management and organizational theorists, posited that "the series of decisions which determines behavior over some stretch of time may be called a strategy" (Simon, 1957, p. 67). Working in this tradition, distinguished McGill University management scholar Henry Mintzberg in his book *Tracking Strategies* defines strategy as "pattern: consistency in behavior over time" (Mintzberg, 2007, p. 1). His management scholarship has focused on patterns of organizational behavior as manifest in observable actions, actions that can be tracked and evaluated for their coherence and impacts as strategy. Management scholars are "tracking strategies" and their results with no grounding in evaluation. Evaluation can learn from what management scholars are doing, but deepen and adapt their approaches and insights to the particular concerns and mandates of the evaluation profession.

Management scholarship and private-sector trends spill over to and affect government, nonprofit, and philanthropic sectors where most evaluation has traditionally occurred. Strategic planning is widely used in all sectors, but tracking strategy as *patterns in organizational behavior* is a relatively recent direction that is having a great deal of influence in the private sector, especially through the writings and consulting of Mintzberg. The *Wall Street Journal* named Henry Mintzberg one of the 10 most influential business thinkers ("Wall Street Journal Most Influential Business Thinkers," 2008), and he was the keynote presenter at the 2008 Evaluation Roundtable mentioned earlier, which explored strategic philanthropy. Mintzberg brings a particularly rich set of ideas about what organizational strategy actually is, how it evolves, and how it affects what people in organizations actually do. Although Mintzberg is well known in the business world, we find that Mintzberg's framework is also applicable and well suited for the work of the public and nonprofit sectors—both in his appreciation of the complexity of the challenges faced and the need to build strong learning and adaptive capacities in order to succeed in these arenas.

Strategy, as Mintzberg defines and tracks it, is different from what evaluators typically mean by a theory of change or conceptualize in a logic model. These differences have significant implications for treating strategy as an evaluand. That is the scope and focus of this volume: *strategy as the evaluand and unit of analysis for evaluation.* Strategy is not what a program or organization plans to do or says it does but rather, what it actually does. Strategy is usually defined as a forward-looking plan for a defined future. Mintzberg's approach is to define strategy as systematic patterns of organizational behavior that determine overall direction, how the organization's work is carried out, and where it is carried out. He distinguishes "intended strategy" from "realized strategy." When examined, "realized strategy" (or what was actually done) reveals patterns of behavior and commitments, the ways that problems are framed, and how an organization relates to the external world. In combination, *these patterns constitute strategy*. Let's take a closer look at Mintzberg's key distinctions and their implications for evaluation.

Strategy Distinctions: Perspective Versus Position

In his teaching, Mintzberg likes to ask, "Was Egg McMuffin, McDonald's breakfast in a bun, a strategic change for the company?" Some respond that it was a strategic change because the innovation constituted a new product aimed at a new market—breakfast eaters. Others say it was a product improvement but not a strategic change because it was still McDonald's fast-food approach (strategy). He calls this "the Egg McMuffin Syndrome"—the failure to distinguish different kinds of change—and evaluators manifest this syndrome every bit as much as business managers and strategic planners.

First, one must distinguish nonstrategic change (improvement within the existing strategy) from strategic change (development of a new direction). Within strategic change, Mintzberg distinguishes changes in *position* from changes in *perspective*. Position focuses on what is done and the territory (landscape, space) in which it is done; for programs this is usually the target population and primary outcomes targeted. Perspective focuses on how something is done; for programs this means how staff work with participants and partners. Egg McMuffin was a strategic change in position (a new product aimed at a new market) but was not a change in perspective, because it still involved producing standardized fast food. Changing a position within perspective, Mintzberg says, is relatively easy because it just involves doing new things in an established way. Changing a position together with a perspective is more significant, for which he offers the imagined example of a gourmet "McDuckling a l'Orange" served at your table instead of picked up at the counter. This kind of change is harder because "perspectives are deeply rooted in organizations, in their cultures" (Mintzberg, 2007, p. 8). But change still comes in response to different environments: After long hesitation, Euro Disney decided to serve wine because the local French population demanded it. McDonald's has begun experimenting with variations based on location: including a crab sandwich on the menu in Maine, serving pastries in France, and brewing gourmet coffee in upscale markets.

Changes in position and perspective can be *either* strategic or nonstrategic. Nonstrategic changes are improvements in implementing the existing strategy. A strategic change, in contrast, constitutes a development—a significant *strategic* departure from business as usual. Mintzberg considers offering a Big Mac on a whole-wheat bun to be a minor product improvement within the same strategic perspective (fast food). Those who prefer whole-wheat to white bread would consider this an improvement, but it is not a significant strategic change in how McDonald's does business.

However, targeting gourmet coffee drinkers represents a strategic change in position, not just an improvement in the way it has served coffee in the past.

Now let us illustrate the distinctions between strategic perspective and strategic position at the program level. Consider an employment program that targets chronically unemployed men of color (its strategic position). Originally, the program planned for generalist staff "coaches" to help men of color locate appropriate training and education in the community (outsourcing all training was its strategic perspective). Improvements in this strategy involved getting better at selecting motivated men of color and supporting coaches to match participants appropriately to training and educational opportunities in the community. Strategic developments, beyond improvements, involved more fundamental changes. Changing the target population to include women and low-income whites occurred, in part because new welfare-to-work legislation during the Clinton administration dramatically increased demand among women on welfare for employment training and the program responded to that increased need and demand (a change in strategic position). This did not involve a change in mission, which remained poverty reduction, but did involve an important change in the program's participant composition. Under Mintzberg's distinctions, this constituted a change in strategic position—a change in target population and outcome (or a change in product, in business terms).

A major developmental change in strategic perspective involved the decision to bring most training in house and create the program's own customized courses because outsourcing just wasn't working. The evaluation feedback from both participants placed in jobs and their employers concluded that available training and education in the community didn't meet the needs of the targeted participants. This led to adding to and changing the staff configuration, hiring trainers, placement specialists, and company recruiters, as well as redefining the role of coaches to specialize in what participants needed at different stages in the program. (That participants needed different kinds of coaching at different stages of the program was an evaluation finding.) Other major strategic developments in perspective involved offering empowerment training for employees already employed in customer companies (not just program participants) and creating a program for men in prison. Framing the evaluation as *evaluating strategy* was well received by the program's leadership and funders because the nonprofit leadership came from the private sector where an emphasis on strategy was greatly valued. Indeed, part of the new program's critique of the existing government, nonprofit, and philanthropic sectors was that they were not sufficiently strategic. The organization's leadership resonated to a focus on evaluating strategy (Patton, 2010, Chapter 2).

Mintzberg's strategic distinctions emphasize that it is important to understand both the degree of change (strategic versus nonstrategic) and the kind of strategic change occurring (position, perspective, or both). Nonstrategic changes are improvements that involve implementing the existing strategy better, for example, more efficiently. Strategic changes are developments in that they involve changes in the organization's focus or way of doing business. Chapter 2 in this volume presents an in-depth example of how the International Development Research Centre used Mintzberg's distinctions as a framework for strategic evaluation. Let's look a bit more closely at these distinctions.

Implications of Taking a Strategic Approach to Evaluation

Mintzberg's strategy distinctions offer a way of engaging with key stakeholders to differentiate important evaluation questions. Evaluating *strategy as perspective* means examining how the organization thinks about itself, including the extent to which the organization's leadership, staff, and participants in the organization's programs articulate a consistent view of strategic perspective. Perspective is the core set of values and theories about how change comes about that shape what an organization is—reflecting its sense of how and where it can be effective. Perspective in the nonprofit sector is often based on its core ideas about how desired social change comes about. We often hear perspective articulated as "going to scale," or "comprehensive community change," or "knowledge development and diffusion," and so on. We would posit that most organizations have perspectives—some weak or strong, but more often than not, largely undeclared and therefore unexamined and untested. Organizations with strong and clear *perspective* can use it to make decisions about where it can work most effectively and how. Clear perspective allows an organization to think about the staff it needs, communicate more effectively with its partners and stakeholders, identify where it can work effectively (or not), and deploy its resources accordingly. The strategic evaluation questions are:

> What is the organization's strategic perspective?
> How aligned are understandings about the organization's strategic perspective across different stakeholder constituencies (leadership, staff, program participants, funders)?

In contrast to strategy as perspective, *strategy as position* focuses attention on where an organization aims to have an effect and contribute to outcomes. In the corporate world, position is where a company can establish a niche-based competitive advantage over others. In the worlds of government, philanthropic, and not-for-profit organizations, strategic position has to do with niche. Debates about strategic position in government focus on what the private sector can and should do, what the public sector can and should do, and what they should do together. In the philanthropic world, foundation executives, board members and staff ask: Why should our foundation do this? Who else is engaged in this arena? What would we bring to it that is different and value added? In the not-for-profit world, strategic position has to do with mission focus versus mission drift, where pursuit of ever-scarce funding can mean following the money wherever it leads regardless of mission.

Strategy as position can productively test how an organization deals with its understanding of its own potential to be effective. Without position it is fairly difficult to even consider an outcomes framework, as position sets the terms of performance—where you will succeed, how much, and in what way. Commitment to a position makes success or failure more obvious than in its absence. The strategic evaluation questions are:

> What is the organization's strategic position?
> How aligned are understandings about the organization's strategic position across different stakeholder constituencies (leadership, staff, program participants, funders)?

Exhibit 1.1 is the evaluation worksheets we used with a group of foundation leaders and evaluators to make distinctions between strategic perspective and strategic position.

Finally, having identified evaluation questions specific to *strategy as perspective* versus *strategy as position*, the next level of evaluation is to look at the relationship between the two. Evaluation questions include:

> What is the relationship between strategic perspective and strategic position?
> How does strategic perspective inform strategic position? To what extent and in what ways does strategic position flow from perspective? What tensions, if any, are manifest between perspective and position? How are these managed?

Figure 1.1 displays this relationship and the evaluation questions that arise from examining the relationship.

Tracking Strategies Over Time: An Evaluation Framework

Another aspect of Mintzberg's work offers an important framework for thinking about, understanding, and engaging in strategy evaluation. Implementing strategy, Mintzberg has found, is inevitably some combination of deliberate and unplanned processes. In studying hundreds of companies over many years, he found that there is no such thing as a perfectly controlled, deliberate process in which intentions lead to formulation of plans, implementation, and the full realization of intended results. The real world doesn't unfold that way. As the graphic in Figure 1.2 shows, realized strategy (where you end up after some period of time) begins as intended strategy (planning), but, not all of what is intended is realized. Some things get dropped or go undone, becoming unrealized strategy. What remains, deliberate strategy, intersects with emergent strategy to become realized strategy. Emergent strategy comes from seizing

Exhibit 1.1. What Is Strategy?

Worksheet # 1: Applying strategy distinctions for evaluation design
Exercise: Apply strategy distinctions and match to evaluation options

Instructions: For your organization, identify and distinguish an example of your strategic perspective and an example of your strategic position. For each, identify the primary evaluation focus and questions. Complete the table below.

	Strategy Story Lines	*Evaluation Approach Matched to Strategy: Identify Evaluation Focus*
Example of your organization's *strategic perspective*	What is the strategy story line (or multiple story lines and points of view) here?	Evaluation focus: Key evaluation questions
Example of your organization's *strategic position*	What is the story line (or multiple story lines and points of view) here?	Evaluation focus: Key evaluation questions

Worksheet # 2: Bringing evidence to bear in evaluating strategy
Data issues and options

Exercise: Identify strategic evaluation *methods and measures*

Instructions: For your organization, having distinguished strategic *perspective* and strategic *position*, and the prospective evaluation focus of each, identify possible methods and measures. Complete the table below.

	Strategies	*Evaluation Approach Matched to Strategy: Identify Key Evaluation Question(s) and Potential Methods/Data to Evaluate the Strategy*

Example of your organization's *strategic perspective*	Differentiate project strategies from overall organization strategies, but examine and articulate their degree of alignment.	1. Review key evaluation questions from previous worksheet.
		
		2. Possible methods/measures
		  a. Project level
		  b. Overall organization level

Example of your organization's *strategic position*	Differentiate project strategies from overall organization strategies, but examine and articulate their degree of alignment.	1. Review key evaluation questions from previous worksheet.
		
		2. Possible methods/measures:
		  a. Project level
		  b. Overall organization level

Figure 1.1. Strategic Perspective in Relation to Strategic Position: Evaluation Questions

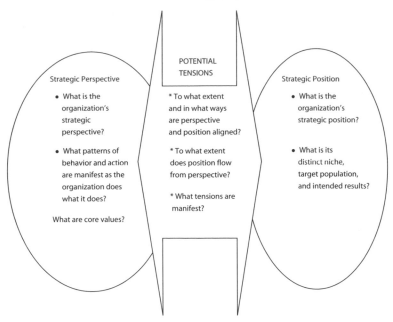

Figure 1.2. An Evaluation Framework for Tracking Strategy

Source: Created from Mintzberg (2007, Chapter 1).

new opportunities, which is a reason some things that were planned go undone as new and better opportunities arise (Mintzberg, 2007, Chapter 1).

These insights about strategy implementation and realization in the real-world contrast significantly with the classic accountability-oriented approach of evaluation in which program implementation and results are measured and judged based on what a program planned to do and achieve (intended outcomes). Under such an accountability framework, an innovative and adaptive program that seizes new opportunities and adjusts to changing conditions will be evaluated negatively. Strategic evaluation, in contrast, expects that some of what is planned will go unrealized, some will be implemented roughly as expected, and some new things will emerge. Strategic evaluation tracks and documents these different aspects of strategic implementation—and their implications for results. This framework generates the following evaluation questions:

What was the intended (planned) strategy?
What aspects of the intended strategy were implemented as planned, becoming *realized strategy*?
What planned strategy elements were dropped? Why?
What unplanned and emergent strategies were implemented, becoming part of realized strategy? Why? How? With what implications?
What has been learned (over some period of time) about the relationships among intended, implemented, dropped, emergent, and ultimately realized strategies? (See Figure 1.2.)

Strategy Evaluation and Learning

If deliberate strategy is about control, emergent strategy is about learning. . . .
Almost every sensible real-life strategy process combines emergent learning
with deliberate control. (Mintzberg, 2007, p. 5)

Mintzberg emphasizes that ongoing attention to strategy should focus on learning and adaptation, not accountability (i.e., whether what was planned was actually implemented as planned with the planned results). In Mintzberg's model, strategy is an ongoing process of venturing and learning that supports how an organization creates strategy over time. "Doing" is the precursor to "learning," and learning is the precursor to developing a robust vision for the work to be done going forward. Planning follows, hopefully based on a strong understanding of the organization—its competencies, how it works best, how it recognizes and appreciates opportunities, and how it gauges situations where goals might be reached. Problems arise when strategy formulation and implementation are treated as separate realities. Too often when a program fails to meet an objective, program execution is blamed, when in reality, he argues, inadequate strategy development, separated in time and place from the actual work, is often the root of the problem. Thus, organizations are strongest when they employ cycles of venturing, learning, and visioning as part and parcel of how strategy is approached. Mintzberg believes that often organizations start with the plan before they know what they can do well and before they have the experience to understand where and how they have succeeded. They need to engage in strategic learning.

Strategic learning has emerged as a way of describing an approach to evaluation that aims at "helping organizations or groups learn in real-time and adapt their strategies to the changing circumstances around them. It means integrating evaluation and evaluative thinking into strategic decision making and bringing timely data to the table for reflection and use. It means making evaluation a part of the intervention—embedding it so that it influences the process" (Coffman, Reed, Morariu, Ostenso, & Stamp, 2010, p. 4). In particular, strategic learning connects evaluation and strategy as explicitly interdependent and mutually reinforcing.

> *Evaluation is a support for strategy.* First and foremost, evaluation must be seen and positioned as a key support for strategy development and management; it should have a seat at the strategy table. Traditionally, evaluation is not viewed in this way. It is considered a separate component, usually entering after a strategy already has been developed or implemented. An emphasis on strategic learning fundamentally changes evaluation's role and positioning. (Coffman et al., 2010, p. 5)

The worldwide battle against polio offers an example in this regard, as well as an illustration of Mintzberg's framework (Figure 1.2) depicting how strategy changes over time. Polio, recently thought to be on the verge of eradication, is once again spreading through countries thought to have completely controlled the disease. This has focused attention on the global health debate about alternative strategies: "Is humanity better served by waging wars on individual diseases, like polio? Or is it better to pursue a broader set of health goals simultaneously—improving hygiene, expanding immunizations, providing clean drinking water—that don't eliminate any one disease, but might improve the overall health of people in developing countries?" (Guth, 2010). Over a period of two decades, the polio eradication campaign has cost $8.2 billion, with The Bill and Melinda Gates Foundation having contributed nearly $1 billion to wipe out the disease.

Fighting individual diseases is a focused, targeted, vertical strategy with clear, specific, and measurable outcomes, the kind of project-oriented approach evaluators have traditionally urged in logic modeling exercises. Improving the overall health care system and population health is a broader, horizontal strategy with less well-defined goals and multifaceted interventions. Such a strategy involves systems change as the broad impact, a complex theory of change that lends itself to a more developmental evaluation approach (Patton, 2010, Chapter 5). The Gates Foundation had been following the vertical strategy, not only in polio but in concentrating on developing vaccines for other diseases. The re-emergence of polio has been interpreted as a failure of the vertical strategy. "Disease-specific wars can succeed only if they also strengthen the overall health system in poor countries" (Guth, 2010).

NEW DIRECTIONS FOR EVALUATION • DOI: 10.1002/ev

[Mr. Gates] built his foundation on the promise of life-saving vaccines, reflecting his penchant toward finding technological solutions to problems. As polio shows, technology can be hampered by political, religious and societal obstacles in the countries where he's spending his money. He's still learning how to navigate through those forces. (Guth, 2010)

The new strategy of the Gates Foundation and world health authorities more generally integrates both vertical and horizontal strategies. This change is an example of how strategic evaluation can support strategic learning.

Strategic Knowledge, Rhetoric, and Behavior: Evaluation Comparisons

H. Igor Ansoff (1918–2002) is considered the father of strategic management ("Management Guru," 2008). The Igor Ansoff Strategy Prize is named in his honor. Max Boisot received the Igor Ansoff Strategy Prize for his influential book, *Knowledge Assets* (Boisot, 1998), in which he examined strategically the important distinctions, important to evaluators, between data, information and knowledge.

Data: discernible differences between alternative states of a system

Information: data that modify the expectations or conditional readiness of an observer

Knowledge: the set of expectations that an observer holds with respect to an event. "It is a disposition to act in a particular way that has to be inferred from behavior rather than observed directly." (Boisot, 1998, p. 21)

These definitions and distinctions call attention to the significance of examining strategy through observed organizational behaviors not just organizational rhetoric. Knowledge is the basis for strategic expectations. A change in knowledge can be expected to alter strategic expectations. "Clearly, knowledge structures—i.e., expectations—are modified by the arrival of new information, and such information, in turn, has to be extracted from the data generated by phenomena" (Boisot, 1998, p. 21).

This dynamic view of strategy is consistent with Mintzberg. Knowledge structures, for Boisot, are the basis for *strategic intent* (Boisot, 1998, pp. 186–187). A classic evaluation comparison, then, would be between expressed strategic intent and actual strategic behavior. Or, expressed more directly: Is the organization walking its strategy talk? And is the organization generating and adapting to new knowledge?

Boisot, like Mintzberg, has emphasized that context matters in understanding how consistent or dynamic strategy is as implementation unfolds. The degree to which an organization's environment is predictable or turbulent affects knowledge generation and adaptation imperatives. Traditional, methodical, and detailed strategic planning works when the environment is relatively knowable, stable, and manageable. However, when the complexity of the environment reduces certainty because of turbulence and lack of definitive knowledge about how to achieve desired results, strategic approaches must be more emergent and flexible. Evaluating strategy would then need to be highly adaptive and developmental (Patton, 2010), matching the evaluation approach to the strategic approach.

Strategy and Policy: Strategic Policy Evaluation

One focus for strategic learning and one question that often emerges in considering strategy as an evaluand is how, if at all, evaluating strategy is different from evaluating policy. Internationally, Aotearoa, New Zealand, evaluators Nan Wehipeihana and Jane Davidson have been working on strategic policy evaluation (Wehipeihana & Davidson, 2010). Drawing on the work of Davidson and Martineau (2007) on strategic uses of evaluation, they differentiate strategic policy evaluation as focusing on "strategic goals and high level outcomes and ultimately, the achievement of the organisation's mission or vision. . . .[This] differs from programme or intervention evaluation primarily with respect to the type and scope of information provided and its intended users. Findings are designed and timed to be useful not only to those implementing the interventions that form part of a strategy, but to those reviewing and reformulating the overarching strategy itself" (Wehipeihana & Davidson, p. 3). Strategic policy evaluation in their framework poses questions that go beyond the evaluation of a single initiative. Examples include:

1.   What is the value of a particular policy initiative as a contributor to strategic policy outcomes?

2.   How well does each initiative fit with and complement the other initiatives that make up the strategic policy mix?

3.   What is the collective value of the suite of initiatives to achieve a particular strategic outcome? (Wehipeihana & Davidson, 2010, p. 4)

What differentiates strategic policy evaluation from just policy evaluation as typically undertaken is the strategic focus on *Big Picture* questions: answering macrolevel cross-project questions. They conclude:

Strategic policy evaluation is about strategically planning to get from evaluation the answers to critical policy questions.

Strategic policy evaluation needs to be a planned, conscious and deliberative process with a focus on policy evaluation—as opposed to assuming that the answers will "fall out of" a series of programme evaluations.

A policy evaluation framework that looks *at* evaluations of individual initiatives and *across* these initiatives as well as mapping up to key outcomes and
strategic goals is a must. (Wehipeihana & Davidson, 2010, p. 20)

This issue includes an example of strategic policy evaluation, the W. K.
Kellogg evaluation of the U.S. policy of *devolution* that shifted much responsibility for welfare-reform decision making from the federal government to
state and local officials. In examining that case example through the lens of
strategy we faced the challenge of differentiating strategy evaluation from
policy evaluation. We settled on, and offer here for your consideration, the
following basis for distinguishing the two: Policy is the content (what is to
be done) and strategy is the process (how it is to be done). In the devolution example, the policy content was welfare rules and regulation. The strategy was how reform decisions would be made (devolution) and how reform
would be implemented (allowing variations and experiments at the state
and local levels). Using these distinctions between policy and strategy,
strategic policy evaluation would be a comprehensive approach that would
examine both what and how, both outcomes and process, both means
and ends.

Strategy Formulation Versus Strategic Execution

In real life, strategy is actually very straightforward.
You pick a general direction and implement like hell.
    Jack Welch, former CEO, General Electric

The final set of evaluation questions we would offer at this point concern strategy development and articulation versus strategy execution. The
field of evaluation has long distinguished between *idea failure* versus *implementation failure*, and emphasized the importance of being able to tell the
difference. When something doesn't work, is it because it's a bad idea (e.g.,
poor theory or weak strategy) or because of bad implementation? Likewise,
in evaluating strategy, it becomes important to look at tensions that arise
between strategy articulation and development versus strategy implementation and execution. "Execution trumps strategy, every time," is the title
of a speech given to the Evaluation Roundtable by Dr. Steven Schroeder, a
former foundation executive, as he recounted his efforts to eradicate
tobacco use in the United States. His greatest lesson in his work on this
campaign was his recognition that *a priori* strategy along with post hoc
evaluation had little to do with the decisions that were made during implementation. Strong execution backed up by solid information was his key to
decision making in his groundbreaking work at the Robert Wood Johnson
Foundation.

NEW DIRECTIONS FOR EVALUATION • DOI: 10.1002/ev

The tension between strategy formulation versus strategy execution has long been the subject of attention and debate in the business world. For many years, the importance of strategic planning and strategy development received primary emphasis. But recent business books have emphasized execution, as in these best-selling titles:

> *Execution: The Discipline of Getting Things Done* (Bossidy, Charan, & Burck, 2002)
> *Execution Premium* (Kaplan & Norton, 2008)
> *Execution Revolution: Solving the One Business Problem That Makes Solving All Other Problems Easier* (Harpst, 2008)

One lesson from these experts is that execution is not a lower-down-in-the-organization issue, whereas strategy is the purview of senior management. Senior management, they argue, has to attend to execution every bit as much as strategy. Therein lies the tension. How to attend to both? And therein reside more evaluation questions for evaluating strategy.

This example illustrates the point of this opening chapter, namely, that the language of strategy provides a particular window into issues of program and organizational effectiveness and opportunities for improvement that make evaluating strategy a special niche worthy of attention. Yes, it would be possible when hearing about issues of strategy formulation versus strategy execution to revert to traditional evaluation language about idea failure versus implementation failure. But that means imposing our language on those with whom we work. If their language and concerns are about strategy, both strategy formulation and strategy execution, then that is the appropriate way to conceptualize and focus the strategic evaluation inquiry. Figure 1.3 presents this relationship graphically.

Strategic Alignment

A common issue that emerges when evaluating strategy concerns the nature and extent of strategic alignment. Is strategic perspective aligned with strategic position? This question was one of the guiding issues that emerged in evaluating the strategy of the International Development Research Centre featured in the next chapter. The findings of the strategic review pointed to the importance of managing tensions between strategic perspective and strategic position as well as tensions between strategy formulation and strategy execution, another arena in which alignment issues arise. A strategic alignment issue for philanthropic foundations is consistency between grant-making strategy and investment strategy (financial investments of the foundation's endowment). Program-related investments, in which endowment funds are invested in accordance with the institution's mission and values, seek to align grant-making and investment strategies. Kramer, Mahmud, and Makka (2010) provide a

Figure 1.3. Strategy Formulation Versus Execution

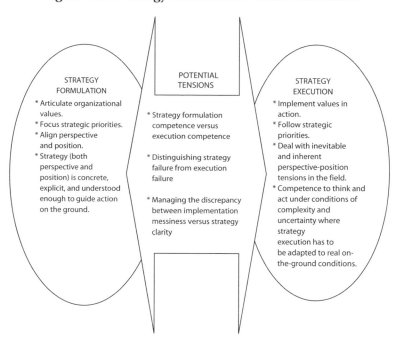

case example of this "integrated strategy for grantmaking and mission investing" in the arena of climate change.

Strategic alignment is one example of a criterion for evaluating strategy. The final chapter in this volume, on methods and measurement issues, provides additional criteria.

Conclusion

> There is always a better strategy than the one you have;
> you just haven't thought of it yet.
>   Sir Brian Pitman, former CEO of Lloyds TSB (Pitman, 2003)

This chapter has suggested that a better strategy for evaluating strategy is to treat strategy as an evaluand. This is especially appropriate for those stakeholders who place a great value on strategic thinking and those organizations where the language of *being strategic* permeates the organizational culture. With this as the basic premise of the chapter, we adapted Mintzberg's framework for distinguishing and tracking strategies to the challenges of evaluating strategy.

Our focus has been on recognition of behavioral and organizational patterns. Strategy is revealed by examining those patterns and evaluation involves, in part, comparing rhetoric about strategy with the behavioral realities of how the organization operates strategically, thereby helping an organization separate the rhetoric from the reality of their work. It is in the dynamic tension between strategy as perspective versus strategy as position that many organizations trip up on in their efforts to be strategic. Perspectives and positions are often at odds as different people at different places in the organization focus on different aspects of strategy. An overarching evaluation question, then, is inquiry into the strategic alignment of various parts of the organization. Evaluating strategy involves evaluating that alignment, including alignment between strategy as articulated versus strategy as actually executed.

In essence, evaluating strategy can be an evaluation strategy. The tactics of evaluation involve a specific design, methods, and measurements. Evaluation strategy concerns overall purpose and intended uses. In being strategic about evaluation, the wisdom of the great Chinese General Sun Tzu on *The Art of War* (6th century B.C.) is germane. He observed:

> Strategy without tactics is the slowest route to victory.
> Tactics without strategy is the noise before defeat.

References

Boisot, M. H. (1998). *Knowledge assets: Securing competitive advantage in the information economy.* New York: Oxford University Press.

Bossidy, L., Charan, R., & Burck, C. (2002). *Execution: The discipline of getting things done.* New York: Crown Business.

Brest, P. (2010, Spring). The power of theories of change. *Stanford Social Innovation Review*, pp. 46–51.

Brest, P., & Harvey, H. (2008). *Money well spent: A strategic plan for smart philanthropy.* New York: Bloomberg Press.

Bryson, J. M. (2004). *Strategic planning for public and nonprofit organizations: A guide to strengthening and sustaining organizational achievement* (3rd ed.). San Francisco: Jossey-Bass.

Buchanan, P., & Buteau, E. (2010, April 22). Should grant makers embrace experts' advice? It all depends. *Chronicle of Philanthropy*, p. 32.

Buteau, E., Buchanan, P., & Brock, A. (2009). *Essentials of foundation strategy.* Cambridge, MA: Center for Effective Philanthropy. Retrieved from http://www.effective philanthropy.org/assets/pdfs/CEP_EssentialsOfFoundationStrategy.pdf

Center for Effective Philanthropy. (2009). *Essentials of foundation strategy.* Cambridge, MA: The Center for Effective Philanthropy. Retrieved from http://www.effectivephil anthropy.org/assets/pdfs/CEP_EssentialsOfFoundationStrategy.pdf

Coffman, J., Reed, E., Morariu, J., Ostenso, L., & Stamp, A. (2010). *Evaluation for strategic learning: Principles, practice, and tools.* Washington, DC: Center for Evaluation Innovation, Innovation Network.

Congressional Research Service. (2007). *State E-government strategies: CRS report to Congress. Identifying best practices and applications.* Washington, DC: Congressional Research Service. Retrieved from http://www.fas.org/sgp/crs/secrecy/RL34104.pdf

David, F. R. (2008). *Strategic management: Concepts and cases* (12th ed.). New York: Prentice Hall.

Davidson, E. J., & Martineau, J. M. (2007). Strategic uses of evaluation. In J. W. Martineau, L. Merritt, & K. Hannum (Eds.), *Leadership development evaluation handbook* (pp. 433–463). San Francisco: Jossey-Bass.

Guth, R. A. (2010, April 23). Gates rethinks his war on polio. *Wall Street Journal.* Retrieved from http://online.wsj.com/article/SB10001424052702303348504575184093239615022 .html?KEYWORDS=Gates+Rethinks+His+War+on+Polio

Haines, S. G. (2007). *The top 10 everyday tools for strategic thinking: Strategic thinking handbook #2.* San Diego: Systems Thinking Press.

Harpst, G. (2008). *Execution revolution: Solving the one business problem that makes solving all other problems easier.* Findlay, OH: Six Disciplines.

Hill, C., & Jones, G. (2009). *Strategic management: An integrated approach* (9th ed.). Florence, KY: South-Western College Publishing.

Hitt, M. A., Ireland, R. D., & Hoskisson, R. E. (2010). *Strategic management: Concepts and cases: Competitiveness and globalization* (9th ed.). Florence, KY: South-Western College Publishing.

International Network on Strategic Philanthropy. (2005, June). Rethinking philanthropic effectiveness. *@lliance magazine.* Retrieved from http://www.alliancemagazine.org/en /content/international-network-strategic-philanthropy-rethinking-philanthropic-effec tiveness

Johnson, R. (2008). The next BIG THING: Strategic performance management. Retrieved from http://www.4hoteliers.com/4hots_fshw.php?mwi=3432

Kaplan, R. S., & Norton, D. P. (2000). *The strategy-focused organization: How balanced scorecard companies thrive in the new business environment.* Boston: Harvard Business School Press.

Kaplan, R. S., & Norton, D. P. (2008). *Execution premium.* Boston: Harvard Business School Press.

Keyne Insight. (2010). *Strategy-driven execution management.* Retrieved from http://www.keyneinsight.com/

Kramer, M., Mahmud, A., & Makka, S. (2010). *Maximizing impact: An integrated strategy for grantmaking and mission investing in climate change.* Boston: FSG Social Impact Advisors. Retrieved from http://www.fsg-impact.org/

La Piana, D. (2008). *Nonprofit strategy revolution: Real-time strategic planning in a rapid-response world.* Saint Paul, MN: Fieldstone Alliance.

Management guru: Igor Ansoff. (2008, July 18). *The Economist.* Retrieved from http://www.economist.com/business-finance/management/displaystory.cfm? story_id=11701586

Mathison, S. (2005). *Encyclopedia of evaluation.* Thousand Oaks, CA: Sage.

Millett, R. (2010, March). The role of evaluation in foundations and the quest for effectiveness. Mary E. Corcoran Keynote address, Minnesota Evaluation Studies Institute Annual Conference, Minneapolis.

Mintzberg, H. (2007). *Tracking strategies.* New York: Oxford University Press.

Mintzberg, H., Lampel, J., & Ahlstrand, B. (2005). *Strategy safari: The complete guide through the wilds of strategic management.* New York: Free Press.

Office of Management and Budget. (2002). *E-government strategy: Simplified delivery of services to citizens.* Washington, DC: Office of Management and Budget. Retrieved from http://www.usa.gov/Topics/Includes/Reference/egov_strategy.pdf

Patton, M. Q. (2010). *Developmental evaluation: Applying complexity concepts to enhance innovation and use.* New York: Guilford Press.

Pearce, J., & Robinson, R. (2010). *Strategic management* (12th ed.). New York: McGraw-Hill/Irwin.

Pitman, B. (2003, April). Leading for value. *Harvard Business Review,* p. 81. Retrieved from http://hbr.org/product/leading-for-value-hbr-onpoint-enhanced-edition/an/340X-PDF-ENG?N=4294841677&Ntt=Contents%252520April%2525202003

Putnam, K. (2010). *What is strategic philanthropy?* Retrieved from http://www.putnam cic.com/pdf/StrategicPhilanthropy.pdf

Simon, H. (1957). *Models of man.* New York: Wiley.

Sloan, J. (2006). *Learning to think strategically.* Woburn, MA: Butterworth-Heinemann.

TopConsultant. (2010). *Management consulting recruitment channel report 2010.* Retrieved from http://www.top-consultant.com/Top-Consultant_2010_Recruitment _Channel_Report.pdf

Walker, R. (1983, October 13). Business philanthropy seen as an investment. *Christian Science Monitor.* Retrieved from http://www.wordspy.com/words/strategicphilan thropy.asp

Wall Street Journal most influential business thinkers. (2008, May 21). *Wall Street Journal.* Retrieved from http://maven.wordpress.com/2008/05/11/wall-street-journal-most-influential-business-thinkers/

Wehipeihana, N., & Davidson, E. J. (2010, May). *Strategic policy evaluation: Answering macro-level cross-project questions.* Presented at Anzea Regional Symposium, Wellington, Aotearoa, New Zealand. Retrieved from http://realevaluation.co.nz/pres/anzea StrategicPolicyEval10.pdf

MICHAEL QUINN PATTON *is founder and director of Utilization-Focused Evaluation, and author of the book by that name. He is a former president of the American Evaluation Association.*

PATRICIA A. PATRIZI *is chair of the Evaluation Roundtable and principal of Patrizi Associates, Philadelphia.*

Wind, T., & Carden, F. (2010). Strategy evaluation: Experience at the International Development Research Centre. In P. A. Patrizi & M. Q. Patton (Eds.), *Evaluating strategy. New Directions for Evaluation, 128*, 29–46.

2

Strategy Evaluation: Experience at the International Development Research Centre

Tricia Wind, Fred Carden

Abstract

This chapter examines how the International Development Research Centre (IDRC) has framed and used strategic evaluations. Drawing from IDRC's experience, the authors look at Henry Mintzberg's ideas on strategy formation, and explore potential implications for evaluation in an organization that resembles what Mintzberg calls an "adhocracy." The International Development Research Centre is a Canadian Crown Corporation that supports research in developing countries and undertakes evaluative work at different levels: strategic evaluations, program and project evaluation, and ongoing learning. "Strategic" evaluations examine issues that cut across the Centre's 18 programs. They have focused on programming modalities and broad corporate result areas like capacity building and policy influence. In a decentralized, utilization-focused approach to evaluation, IDRC has taken the view that strategic-level evaluation requires separate studies, as opposed to rolling up data from program or project evaluations. © Wiley Periodicals, Inc., and the American Evaluation Association.

The views expressed are those of the authors and do not necessarily reflect the views of the IDRC.

Editors' Introduction

*A*s independent evaluation consultants, the editors worked with the International Development Research Centre (IDRC) to conduct a strategic review of that organization's work over a 5-year period. That strategic review is cited and discussed in this chapter, and it was as a result of that review that we invited the authors to prepare this chapter. Indeed, our work with IDRC provided important impetus for proposing this volume of New Directions for Evaluation on evaluating strategy.

IDRC has long served as an exemplar of an organization that takes evaluation seriously. For example, the fourth edition of Utilization-Focused Evaluation features IDRC as a case example of evaluation excellence stating: "Nowhere are evaluative thinking and mainstreaming evaluation as integral to organizational culture better illustrated than in the Corporate Assessment Framework of the International Development Research Centre" (Patton, 2008, p. 158). IDRC's strategic approach to evaluation was also featured in a previous volume of NDE (Carden & Earl, 2007) on process use in theory, research, and practice. One of the authors of this chapter, Fred Carden, Director of Evaluation at IDRC, has written a book on how knowledge influences policy in development contexts, an approach that exemplifies strategic thinking about research and evaluation use (Carden, 2009). In this chapter you are offered an inside look at how a major organization and its evaluation unit have approached evaluating strategy. This isn't a theoretical look at what evaluating strategy might entail. This is a real-world case example of evaluating strategy and using the thinking and findings that flowed from the strategic evaluation in setting the future direction for the organization and its programs.

Evaluation at the International Development Research Centre (Canada)

Evaluating strategy takes different forms in different organizations. This article describes the International Development Research Centre (the Centre) of Canada, and how evaluation functions within it. It describes the Centre's experience of using strategic evaluations to address result areas and programming modalities that cut across Centre programming—evaluations that address elements of the Centre's corporate strategy. The Centre has taken the view that evaluations at this level require separate studies, as opposed to aggregating, or "rolling up" data from projects or programs. In reflecting on strategic evaluations, and evaluating at the level of Centre strategy, the article summarizes a recent paper written by Patricia Patrizi and Michael Patton that has become influential for self-assessment, external evaluation, and strategic planning. That paper uses the work of Henry Mintzberg on strategy, and this article goes further to consider implications for evaluation at the level of strategy for one of the four organizational types that Mintzberg identifies—the adhocracy organization.

NEW DIRECTIONS FOR EVALUATION • DOI: 10.1002/ev

The International Development Research Centre is a public corporation established by an Act of Parliament of the Government of Canada 40 years ago. The Centre builds the capacity of people and organizations in developing countries to undertake the research that they identify as most urgent. IDRC's purpose is to help developing countries use science and technology to find practical, long-term solutions to the social, economic, and environmental problems they face. Our support is directed toward creating a local research community whose work will build healthier, more equitable, and more prosperous societies.

This is a large mandate and the Centre focuses its efforts through support to research in four program areas: agriculture and the environment; health and health systems; social and economic policy; and science, technology, and innovation. IDRC supports research in developing countries in sub-Saharan Africa, the Middle East and North Africa, Latin America and the Caribbean, South Asia, and Southeast and East Asia. In some of our work we join forces with other donors, both Canadian and international, to increase the resources going towards research that addresses the needs of developing countries. The Centre's program staff does much more than fund research; they actively work with researchers to strengthen their research skills from the design stage of a project through to supporting the use of research results for development. The Centre's intent is to build capacity in the global south and support research on development in the global south primarily led by southern researchers.

In order to be effective in achieving these objectives, the Centre strives to be an accountable, learning organization. It does this by integrating a culture of "evaluative thinking" into its activities (IDRC, 2007). Evaluative thinking involves being results oriented, reflective, questioning, and using evidence to test assumptions. It is manifested through program-based activities that, for example, make use of dialogue-based project completion reports (Carden & Earl, 2007) to reflect on successes, failures, and learning in projects, both regarding the research supported and the role of the IDRC staff person. It is manifested as well through cross-program activities that share experience and results around a specific issue. For example, the Annual Learning Forum (see IDRC, 2006), organized by the Evaluation Unit and Programs Branch, has used monitoring and evaluation data to explore the Centre's experience in building organizational capacity of research organizations. This year, the Annual Learning Forum focuses on learning more about monitoring and evaluation.

Evaluation plays an important role in building and sustaining this culture. Evaluation begins at the planning stage when the intended results are articulated in the Corporate Strategy and Program Framework (CSPF) and in each program prospectus (its 5-year plan) that are approved by the Centre's Board of Governors.

The Centre's framework for evaluation is utility: evaluation should have a clear use and should respond to the needs of the user, whether management, a program, or a partner. The Centre's approach to evaluation prioritizes equally the use of rigorous methods and the utility of the evaluation process and findings. As a result, the Centre and its Evaluation Unit do not advocate or employ any particular evaluation content, model, method, theory, or even use. The Centre's approach to evaluation mirrors its approach to research for development, which also supports many types of research questions, using different methods and for numerous uses.

Evaluation at the Centre is decentralized. This means that decisions about what, when, and how to evaluate are shared across different layers within the organization, and evaluations are conducted as close as possible to the key users. Project evaluations are managed by program staff or partner organizations. Programs lead their own evaluations for their learning and accountability needs. Centre-wide evaluations and evaluations for IDRC's Board are managed by the Evaluation Unit. The Unit is an internal evaluation function. As such, the evaluation function is housed in the Corporate Strategy branch; its main client is program staff in Programs and Partnership Branch. The Unit manages a modest programming budget, which permits it to both conduct evaluations and support research and capacity building on evaluation.

As noted in the Special Examination of the Centre by the Auditor General for Canada (2008), building a strong culture of evaluative thinking requires that evaluation go beyond the conduct and promulgation of evaluation studies. The Evaluation Unit, Programs and Partnership Branch, and southern researchers are all actively involved in these efforts. First, supporting the use of evaluation means that the Centre is actively involved in the development of fora for reflecting on findings such as the Annual Learning Forum mentioned above. Second, the Centre and project partners develop evaluation tools and methods relevant to development research, especially as the field moves beyond project evaluation to address more strategic issues. Third, building evaluation capacity is a key component of supporting a critical, reflective, and learning culture—not only within the Centre but also with research-partner organizations. Strengthening the field of evaluation in the south is critical if evaluation is to take hold effectively in our partner organizations. In these ways, evaluation becomes a dimension of organizational development, knowledge systems, and evidence-based decision making. Two external reviews of the Evaluation Unit (Byrne, Davies, & Kumar, 2010; Love, 2005) have confirmed that evaluative thinking is strong throughout the Centre, and that the Centre's evaluation model has served the organization well.

In addition to project- and program-level evaluations, the Centre has always conducted what it calls "strategic evaluations." These are evaluations that address an issue of critical importance to the Centre in fulfilling its mandate. These strategic evaluations are the origins and basis of strategy evaluation at the Centre.

Strategic Evaluation

The Evaluation Unit was established in late 1991 and has struggled since with the question of how to evaluate at the corporate level. The Unit's primary approach has been to focus on what we call "strategic evaluations." These are defined as evaluations that address issues of concern to the organization as a whole and that contribute to programming in more than one program area and more than one region. They relate directly to one of the primary objectives of the Centre (building capacity for research in the global south and supporting research on development problems of significance in the global south) or to the mechanisms in use at the Centre to achieve these ends (support to networks of researchers, for example).

Strategic evaluations fulfill several objectives. First, they provide evidence of the success and failure of Centre efforts in a particular area. Second, they provide insights into how to improve the ways we work. Learning from strategic evaluations is seen in how new projects or initiatives are designed. Third, they strengthen the evaluative culture of the Centre through building a common approach to a way of working or understanding how we work. Evidence can be seen in the application of concepts and frameworks from strategic evaluations in more than one program area by senior managers (IDRC, 2010, pp. 9–10). Any one strategic evaluation may fulfill one or more of these uses.

Over the past nearly 20 years, 16 strategic evaluations have been carried out by the Evaluation Unit (see Table 2.1). They have been of two main types:

1. Centre-wide studies of major issues
2. Targeted studies

The Centre-wide studies tend to focus on the main modalities and major objectives of the Centre and cut across program areas. In terms of modalities, the Centre has always placed great emphasis on research networks. Because we are working in environments and on thematics in which the number of researchers is small and they are often isolated from one another, IDRC program staff work to connect researchers in networks and build community among them so they can learn from each other, bring new ideas back into their own research, and collaborate on broader topics and comparative research. As a result, networking is centrally important to the Centre and has been the subject of three strategic evaluations, in 1991, 1996, and 2005. A significant number of other studies of individual networks or groups of networks have also been undertaken by programs over the past 20 years.

Capacity building, a key result area for the Centre, is another strategic evaluation topic that's been revisited different times, in different ways. It was a central theme in the Project Leader Tracer Study, it was one of the result

Table 2.1. Strategic Evaluations at the Centre: Year Completed

Centre-wide	Targeted Studies
Networks: 1991	Project effectiveness: 1993
Canadian partnerships: 1994	Secretariats: 1998
Project Leader Tracer Study: 1995	Navrongo: 1998
Cooperative projects: 1995	Competitive grants: 2008
Participatory research: 1995	Devolution: 2009
Networks: 1996	Strategy evaluation: 2009
Networks: 2005	
Capacity building: 2008	
Policy influence: 2009	
Large conferences: 2009	

areas of research networks, and then was the focus of a large-scale study that finished in 2009. The capacity-building study pushed the analysis from individual research teams and their capacities for research, into organizational capacity development, further than the previous studies did. The latest strategic evaluation on capacity building solidified earlier work, helped develop frameworks to understand capacity development, and adapted international good practice for capacity development to the Centre's work and approach.

A second example of a strategic evaluation of a major result area is the study of the influence of Centre-supported research on public policy. This study took as its starting point the general observation in the Centre's operating strategy for the period 2000–2005, that the Centre "will foster and support the production, dissemination and application of research results leading to policies and technologies that enhance the lives of people in developing countries" (IDRC, 2000).

In Table 2.1 we noted an evolution in strategic evaluations over time. The Centre-wide studies in the 1990s tended to be fairly focused and took a relatively short period of time to complete, 1 or 2 years. The evaluation processes did not include extensive involvement by a large number of program staff. In contrast, the capacity building and the policy influence studies were completed in 2008 and 2009, respectively, but both these studies were multiyear, multicomponent studies. Initial work started in 2002, and interim outputs of these evaluations were produced and used from 2004 onwards. However, the last outputs were finalized after several years of work. A second characteristic of the more recent Centre-wide studies is that they are highly process oriented. That is, the staff of the Centre and often researchers supported by the Centre were actively engaged at various stages of the studies. These were not complex multiyear studies completed by the Evaluation Unit independently and then presented to the Centre for information and use. The approach included active engagement, which led to findings being acted upon even before the studies were completed. It is noteworthy that the Cooperative Projects study and the Participatory Research study were less cited and used on completion, although they were not challenged methodologically; they simply did not resonate in the same way as studies in which staff had been actively engaged.

Although each strategic evaluation has been different, most studies share common design phases. The first phase identifies the topic, uses, and users of the evaluation. Topics arise from questions and issues in programs, in consideration of corporate result areas and modalities described in the corporate strategy. The Evaluation Unit works with Programs and Partnership Branch and Centre management to define the topic, identify primary evaluation users, and refine the evaluation questions. The Evaluation Unit convenes an advisory user group to steer the evaluation process. Phase Two provides background information for the evaluation. This starts with gathering what IDRC already knows about the topic, using previous evaluation material and existing documentation. Background research also draws together what others outside IDRC have learned on the topic. These background pieces, often in consultation with sectoral experts, lead to the development of definitions and conceptual frameworks that inform the design and analysis of the evaluation. The primary research for the evaluation is Phase Three. This has included a range of methods. In some cases, evaluations use a broad survey; in others, they are built on a comparative case study method. Evaluation users are gathered to help validate the evaluation findings. Case studies are synthesized through cross-case analysis. The dissemination phase comes next. Strategic evaluations have included a set of activities and outputs to allow users to engage with the findings—meetings, workshops, case study briefs, or communication pieces for different users. In a final phase, studies have fed into guides for programming, and assessment frameworks for future evaluation. In some cases, the last steps were done outside the formal evaluation process, and may be done by partners outside IDRC.

Table 2.1 also illustrates a gap in strategic evaluations at the Centre. From 1998 through 2005, no strategic evaluations were completed. In those years, the staff of the Evaluation Unit was heavily engaged in the development of outcome mapping (Earl, Carden, & Smutylo, 2001) for several years. As the intense period of methodological work subsided, we went back into more Centre-wide and targeted strategic evaluation. But, as noted above, some of the strategic evaluations begun took many years to complete.

The targeted studies reflect a specific need that the Centre had. For example, the Project Effectiveness study looked at several factors such as project size and their effects on workload. This was part of a Centre-wide discussion on the merits of moving to larger projects. The evaluation looked at whether size was the major factor in workload associated with a project (the assumption being that one larger project was less labor intensive than two smaller ones). We found that aside from size, project duration was essential to consider: a large short project was significantly labor intensive, whereas a long-term small project was not. A more recent example of a targeted study came from a request from senior managers for an evaluation of the devolution of international research secretariats that were initially housed within IDRC, but were "devolved" into independent organizations, or programs within other organizations (Armstrong & Khan, 2009). The rationale for conducting the study was that IDRC has always incubated organizations and wanted to know more in the context of learning for future incubations and devolutions.

A characteristic of these targeted studies is that they emerge from quite direct questions. These may be from recommendations in internal reviews the Centre has carried out (as in the case of our study of secretariats supported by IDRC), by direct request from senior managers (as in the case of the study of devolution), or as a contribution to a Centre debate (such as the Navrongo study and the Project Effectiveness study).

A second characteristic is that the targeted studies present much more variable degrees of participation. Because they are more targeted, they tend to be much more focused on answering a specific need that is often more a matter of research and assessment than of engagement during the implementation of the evaluation. The EU still made a priority of facilitating opportunities for Centre staff to engage with the findings.

Strategy Evaluation and Strategic Evaluation

As we noted above, IDRC has struggled with the concept of evaluation at the level of corporate strategy. The path we have chosen does not try to deal with the organization's performance as a whole and we have not tried to roll up standard measures from projects. An analysis of the Corporate Strategy 2005–2010 confirmed that the strategy was not evaluable as a whole. Rather it serves as guidance to programs, each of which operates in its own way. It lays out the Centre's overall way of working, its general objectives and approach. The rationale for this is that programming at the Centre evolves over time and evolves at a different pace in each program. Innovation and research in diverse program areas cannot be centrally planned to any degree of certainty. Some programs reflect entry into a new field of study; others reflect persistence in research in a particular area; still others reflect modest evolution in the field of research under study. Because the level of what is known and unknown in each field varies, what can and should be assessed also varies.

As the analysis below makes clear, a review of the Centre's performance against Mintzberg's framework illustrated the program-level focus of strategy at IDRC. As such, the focus in strategic evaluation on the broad parameters within which the Centre operates provides the most helpful advice for both understanding the achievement of the broad mandate outlined in the Centre's Act (1970) and for helping improve the effectiveness of programming.

The next part of this chapter will explore our understanding of Mintzberg's approach to strategy and how we think it informs evaluation at the Centre.

Evaluating at the Level of Strategy

How do you evaluate at the level of strategy? The objectives in the IDRC Corporate Strategy were quite broad, making evaluating against them difficult. As the Centre approached the planning period for its next 5-year strategy, the EU looked at the question again, hoping that the results would assist the Centre in developing more "evaluable" strategies in this next programming period (2010–2015).

As mentioned in the introduction to this chapter, the Evaluation Unit engaged with Patricia Patrizi and Michael Patton to review recent program and strategic evaluations in light of the Centre's corporate strategy. They focused on the questions: "How does program performance reflect strategy and how has strategy affected program performance?" (Patrizi & Patton, 2009).

The authors approached the task with the use of Mintzberg's 4 Ps of strategy:

the *plan* as written,
the *perspective* of who you are and what you do,
the *position* of where you invest regionally and thematically, and
the *patterns* of behavior and results that actually take place, regardless of what was written down.

Mintzberg argues that a strategy is almost never fully implemented as written. During implementation, some of the written strategy is set aside (unrealized strategy). Realized strategy is a mixture of the written strategy that is accomplished, and the emergent strategy that develops as you go.

The *plans* Patrizi and Patton analyzed were the IDRC Corporate Strategy and the prospecti (5-year plans) of the five programs that had recently been evaluated. From the Corporate Strategy, the authors noted three key parts of IDRC's strategic *perspective*—IDRC builds research capacity, supports research that influences policy, and builds fields of knowledge. They found the corporate strategy gave little indication of strategic *position*—although it names broad program areas and a number of geographic areas, it does not tell programs where and with whom to invest. Decisions of geographic scope, scale, types of institutions, and partners are left to the programs.

Analyzing the connections between written strategy and actual performance as assessed in program and strategic evaluations, Patton and Patrizi found *patterns* of how IDRC strategy plays out in practice. In doing so, they identified several "tensions" in IDRC strategy. They use the word *tensions*:

(. . .) to communicate the long-recognized organizational wisdom that the pursuit of multiple and competing values, ends, and benefits inevitably gives rise to challenges about how to achieve balance. *Tension,* as we use it here, is a descriptive term, not meant to imply judgment. As we worked with the material, we came to understand that the pulls in different directions evidenced by what we saw, is best captured by the concept of "tension." Identifying tensions and making them explicit creates an opportunity to learn from them and become more intentional and effective in managing them. Tensions are largely not resolvable; they exist because of pressures (internal or external) or vested stakes in their existence. Nor can *perfect or even optimal* balance necessarily be achieved as missions tend to drive organization sentiment around maximizing performance and inevitably constrained resources limit balance and effectiveness. Indeed, what constitutes "balance" can change as conditions and situations change, so too with what constitutes effectiveness. Being alert to tensions and, importantly, their consequences, can enhance execution of strategy. (Patrizi & Patton, 2009, p. 5)

The first tension is inherent in the Centre's perspective, between building local research capacity in the global south, and in supporting research that influences policy. They found that program reviews sought evidence for research capacity outcomes in the number and quality of research outputs (typically peer reviewed) and in academic promotion. However, those measures have little to do with policy influence. Research skills are not the same as policy influence skills. Peer-reviewed publications are typically not on policy-makers' reading lists. Policy briefs do not factor into academic promotion. Perhaps most fundamentally, knowledge is only one factor that influences policy processes. A single project can produce both peer-reviewed publications and policy briefs, of course, and good science can influence policy—but the paper drew out the degree to which the drivers and evidence for research capacity assessments go in quite a different direction than those for policy influence.

The report found that IDRC's corporate strategy offered a large range of locations and fields of investment, without clarifying how decisions on strategic position should be made throughout the organization. This could be interpreted as providing room for programs to make those decisions in a decentralized way, or it could leave them waffling on how to make the decision. Their analysis of program reviews suggested the lack of clarity and guidance on position allowed programs to go off in many directions at once, stretching themselves in unproductive ways. Moreover, they found a number of other overlapping tensions within the program reviews that stemmed from the tensions within and across the strategic perspectives and positions of the corporate strategy.

The Patrizi and Patton paper has proved useful to different groups in the Centre. The analysis resonated with senior managers, who found it particularly helpful in two ways: The paper was a clear means to clarify the tensions that exist in programming. It legitimated, as part of strategy, the concept that there are sometimes not either/or choices and approaches but

NEW DIRECTIONS FOR EVALUATION • DOI: 10.1002/ev

a need to balance competing demands and pressures. Second, the paper was the basis for a discussion on the importance of strategy at the program level and the Centre's broader strategic framework (2010–2015). It helped articulate the importance of strategic choices in each program, confirmed that variety in choice was valid—according to the context and needs of each program, and confirmed support of the Centre within the broad parameters of the strategic framework. Program leaders also discussed the paper and its implications.

Concretely, we've seen evidence of uptake in three ways: in external evaluations, in self-assessments by programs on their own strategies, and in the most recent set of 5-year program prospecti. The next few paragraphs illustrate these uses.

The external evaluation of the peace, conflict, and development (PCD) program picked up on the ideas of tensions in a similar way to Patton and Patrizi, and identified specific tensions facing the PCD program. It found evidence of PCD grappling with three tensions in decisions about which partners with whom to engage. On the one hand, the program sought to build the research capacity of organizations in order to strengthen the field in the global south, so they worked with "lesser known or new organizations engaged in peacebuilding research and action" (Reychler, Sharbatke-Church, Thomas, Clegg, & Heilman, 2010). At the same time, the program wished to produce high-quality research, which was more quickly and easily produced by researchers with high existing capacity. On policy influence, the review found the program trying to balance a tension between working with those who produced high-quality research but were not necessarily well placed to influence policy, and "working with actors well situated for policy influence but with limited research experience" (Reychler et al., 2010). The review noted that for PCD, a tension also existed between working with organizations whose primary attention was to producing research versus organizations whose primary intention was to promote change. The review notes that "(a)ttention needs to be given to ensuring that crucial programming decisions . . . embodies this tension between research and change in a way that honours the utility of both" (Reychler et al., 2010).

The Centre's current approach to external reviews of programs starts with the program offering a 25-page self-assessment of its strategic decisions, major research findings, outcomes, and lessons. This is based on their experience in implementing the 5-year prospectus approved by the Centre's Board of Governors. The Patrizi–Patton paper has provided fodder for a number of these reports to reflect on the degree to which the tensions named therein, or others, are evident in their programming and what they are learning as a result. An Information and Communication Technology for Development program self-report (Acacia Programming Initiative, 2010) found no tension between supporting high-quality research and achieving policy influence; rather, these two objectives were seen as mutually reinforcing. In the final self-assessment report of the Evaluation Unit (Evaluation Unit,

2010), the Unit team found that it had, over the life of our program, constantly managed a tension between deliberate programming and being responsive to the demands of our boundary partners within and outside the organization. In each case, reflection on key tensions allowed the program to surface and assess choices that it made.

Finally, evidence of the influence of the Patrizi–Patton paper is seen in the latest set of 5-year program plans approved by the Centre's Board of Governors. In consultations with Michael Patton, program managers decided to include explicit descriptions of their strategic perspectives and positions within written plans. The annotated outline programs followed for drafting their 5-year plans referred to the paper and encouraged programs to consider the tensions as they drafted their programming strategies and approaches. As one example, the Agriculture and Food Security program referred directly to the tensions from the original report and proposed how it will begin to address them. The prospectus commits the program to reviewing both these and emergent tensions partway through its programming period "to identify lessons and update management practices." As with other uses of the Patrizi–Patton report, programs identified other tensions particular to their programming in their prospecti.

In each of these examples, the study of corporate-level strategy was taken back down to the level of programs.

The Centre's Approach to Strategy: Implications for Evaluation

In this section, we look at Henry Mintzberg's ideas on strategy formation within organizations and explore potential implications for evaluation. Our reflections will be limited to what we have observed within the Centre. Mintzberg's book, *Tracking Strategy*, lays out four organizational types:

1. *The machine organization:* In a machine organization, strategy is centrally planned and programmed. The organization is geared for mass production and service, and operates in a fairly stable environment. The parts of the organization are tightly integrated through a formal design.
2. *The entrepreneurial organization:* In entrepreneurial organizations, strategy is led by the vision of the entrepreneur or small group of entrepreneurs. These organizations tend to work in a dynamic environment, and the parts of the organization closely follow the direction set by the leaders.
3. *The professional organization:* A professional organization is a loose collection of individuals who pursue their own work fairly independently, as in a university department. Strategy is formulated by the individual professionals who work within it, and there is little collective learning or control.
4. *The adhocracy organization:* An adhocracy is an organization geared for innovation, operating and responding to a dynamic environment, in

which expert-led teams are loosely coupled. Strategy tends to be more emergent as opposed to being centrally set. Strategy formation is decentralized. It emerges from the strategic venturing of teams into innovative projects and processes, and learning from that venturing.

Although no organization is a pure type, the Centre corresponds most closely to an adhocracy. The term *adhocracy* is problematic because it connotes a one-off process designed for a specific purpose without consideration of broader application. In colloquial use, ad hoc has the sense of being ill-defined and improvised without much thought. In Mintzberg's terms, this is not the case. Rather, an adhocracy is sensitive to and defined by its context. Therefore, an adhocracy is an innovative organization that operates in a complex and changing environment, undertakes many unique activities in response to a common goal, is populated by experts in specialized units, often following different formats and styles of work, and structures its elements in response to the contexts in which that part of the organization is operating. The Centre is shaped by the vision of its founders, but is decentralized into programs that support multidisciplinary action-oriented research on issues in international development. Consistent with Mintzberg's description, the Centre responds more to its environment than to an internally defined central plan. Mintzberg noted, ". . . the functioning of adhocracy really comes down mainly to the interplay between organization and environment. . .We might conclude that the experts of the adhocracy take their lead from the environment, and then seek to fashion their responses to it" (2007, p. 353). For the Centre, the environment to which the organization responds is research agendas in the outside world, predominantly defined by the south, though influenced as well by our existence as a Canadian Crown Corporation, and opportunities in the world of development research.

Mintzberg argues that strategy processes in organizations use a mix of "art, which is about creative insights, and is rooted in the imagination, usually of an individual; craft, which is about practical learning as rooted in experience, often shared by many people; and science, which is about systematic evidence, and is rooted in analysis, often carried out by specialized experts" (2007, pp. 362–363). Mintzberg places these in a triangle, showing the kind of strategy process associated with different mixtures of art, craft, and science in devising strategy. Moreover, the different types of organizations tend to use different kinds of strategy processes (see Figures 2.1 and 2.2). Based on its experience of trying out innovations in either perspective or position (strategic venturing) an adhocracy is "most inclined to *learn* its way into new strategies" (p. 353) in a decentralized way. In the triangles he draws, adhocracies are mostly associated with "craft," that is, devising.

Henry Mintzberg does not address the role of evaluation in these different types of organizations, or how evaluation connects with strategy.

NEW DIRECTIONS FOR EVALUATION • DOI: 10.1002/ev

Figure 2.1. Strategy Process as Art, Craft, and Science

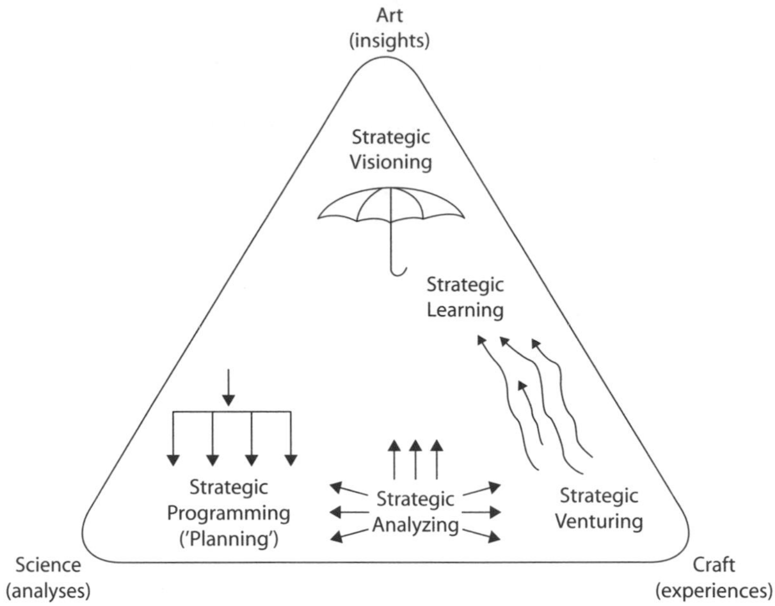

Source: Mintzberg (2007, p. 363).

However, we would suggest some implications for evaluation. Mintzberg's language certainly has many overlaps with evaluation. Analysis, learning, systematic evidence, and experience-based reflection are common to how we describe what evaluation offers. Mintzberg's use of analysis as the "systematic evidence (. . .) rooted in analysis, often carried out by specialized experts" describes well certain kinds of evaluation, such as random control trials. At the same time, different kinds of evaluation allow the practical learning based in experience necessary to develop strategy from an organization's craft. And evaluation processes can facilitate shared analysis, reflection, and learning within a group.

We will examine potential implications for evaluation in adhocracies in more depth, based on the experience of evaluation at the Centre. Applying the Mintzberg framework is a useful tool for understanding, and potentially improving, strategic evaluation at the Centre.

In adhocracies, if strategy is more emergent than centrally planned, evaluation should accompany emergent learning. It should also be geared to the decentralized level at which strategy is actually worked out. As outlined above, at the Centre, that level is programs—that is, not at the level of the organization as a whole. Evaluation at the Centre has been decentralized since the Evaluation Unit was created (Evaluation Unit, 1992). Annual Corporate Evaluation Reports going back to 1994 describe the decentralized evaluation system. Designing a decentralized evaluation system was a

Figure 2.2. Strategy Renewal in the Four Forms of Organization

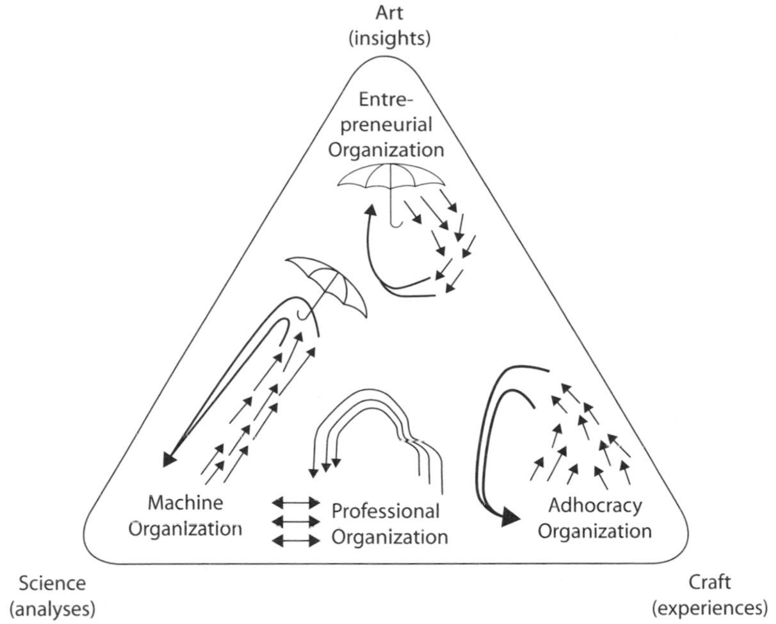

Art
(insights)

Entre-
preneurial
Organization

Machine
Organization

Professional
Organization

Adhocracy
Organization

Science
(analyses)

Craft
(experiences)

Source: Mintzberg (2007, p. 373).

result of wishing to infuse a utilization-focused approach that prioritized using evaluation for programming. In that sense the system took account of emergence, though that term was not discussed at the time. nor did it serve as the design principle.

As seen in Figure 2.2, Mintzberg puts strategy formulation in an adhocracy along the craft and art side of the triangle, aligned to strategic venturing and learning. This implies that evaluation at the Centre should be specifically honed to keep track of strategic venturing, and ensure learning from that venturing is fed back into further crafting of strategy. And, as strategy tends to be more emergent in an adhocracy, evaluation should accompany emergent outcomes. Thus, although predefining evaluation plans and specific assessment measures against corporate-level indicators in a machine organizations might make sense, and would indeed be quite helpful, it may be neither feasible nor useful in an adhocracy. It certainly could not be as specific as it could be in a machine organization. Moreover, an adhocracy's evaluation would not have a singular agenda or focus, as a machine or entrepreneurial organization might. Measurement of progress therefore has to take the various elements of the organization into account and has to identify the various boundaries and focus on strengthening elements as a way to strengthen the whole.

In some ways, we can see this in the strategic evaluation of capacity building. The evaluation started with the Centre's longstanding focus—individual capacity-building efforts with teams of researchers, focused on research skills and skills involved with bringing research into use to influence for policy, practice, behavior change, innovation processes, and the like. However, the strategic evaluation moved on to organizational capacity development—a much broader approach to working with the organization as a whole, not just the research teams within it. During the implementation of the strategic evaluation, the Centre had begun to venture with significantly larger investments than it had before into this form of capacity development. The Centre had launched a new program that provides core grants and significant organizational development investments in policy think tanks. As that program was ramping up, the strategic evaluation took stock of past experiences of organizational capacity building to see what had resulted and what could be learned.

As an adhocracy, the Centre is attuned to its environment but remains flexible and adaptive—"each [project] is a problem-solving exercise, the object of which is to get things right by the end, not at the beginning. If it guessed wrong, it simply adapts" (Mintzberg, 2007, p. 354). The advantages of this approach in a research funding organization are many. The explicit understanding that knowledge is being generated, that we do not yet know, is foundational for IDRC and its researchers. The ability to adapt is essential in the search for knowledge. Mintzberg notes, however, that the risk for the adhocracy is that it adapts too much as the environment changes and goes with "what was fashionable at the time" (p. 356). Importantly, Mintzberg notes that although adhocracies operate in a highly decentralized manner, they can move in an apparently well-organized and coherent fashion— what he calls the wisdom of the crowd and what we would identify as organizational culture and organizational learning. Mintzberg suggests that in order to understand how strategy is crafted in an adhocracy, it is important to try to get into the collective mind of the organization. In some ways, this is also seen in strategic evaluations. Both background research phases and cross-case analysis reports have been geared to uncover IDRC mental models, surface implicit definitions, and build shared language around topics of importance across the Centre.

Perhaps the currently popular terms in evaluation these days—simple, complicated, and complex (Westley, Zimmerman, & Patton, 2006)—might be helpful in this discussion as well. Analysis has connotations of generating certain evidence of contexts and results. In this case, analysis might align with the kinds of evaluations that are geared to simple questions, results, and contexts, where causal links are known or knowable. However, evaluations of experience-based craft may align better with questions, interventions, and results that are socially or technically complicated, or complex.

In his external review of the Evaluation Unit, Arnold Love wrote, "One of the axioms of internal evaluation is that the model should match the organizational context" (2005, p. 24). He described the character of evaluation and the Evaluation Unit within the Centre and drew out its close alignment with the character of the Centre. In thinking about Mintzberg's description of organizational types and potential implications for evaluation within one of those types, we go deeper into Love's axiom. Mintzberg's description of strategy formation, development, and renewal in organizations lets us think further of how to align the internal evaluation function within the Centre to the type of organization it is.

Conclusions

Strategy evaluation in an adhocracy takes on a very different character from that in other organizational types. The nature of an adhocracy is such that thinking about the organization as a coherent whole is not the most useful way to understand its work. What is crucial is to understand the culture of the organization but to assess its strategy through an examination of how it implements the various components of its work. In this way, the strategic evaluations conducted at the Centre are highly consistent with the level and nature of strategy evaluation at the Centre. They cannot be rolled up to a singular picture of how the Centre functions, precisely because it does not function as a singular unit but rather builds its strength through the flexibility it maintains in responding to the unique conditions of the different research domains in which it works, as well as the different regions and conditions in which it operates.

References

Acacia Programming Initiative. (2010). *Acacia 2006–2010 final report*. Ottawa: IDRC.

Armstrong, J., & Khan, A. (2009). *Evaluation of IDRC's experience with the devolution of international secretariats*. Retrieved from http://www.idrc.ca/en/ev-145960–201–1-DO_TOPIC.html

Auditor General for Canada. (2008). *Special examination report: The International Development Research Centre*. Retrieved from http://www.idrc.ca/en/ev-123253–201–1-DO_TOPIC.html

Byrne, A., Davies, I. C., & Kumar, A. K. S. (2010). *Report on the 2010 external review of the IDRC Evaluation Unit*. Ottawa: IDRC.

Carden, F. (2009). *Knowledge to policy: Making the most of development research*. Ottawa & Delhi: IDRC & Sage.

Carden, F., & Earl, S. (2007). Infusing evaluative thinking as process use: The case of the International Development Research Centre. *New Directions for Evaluation, 116*, 61–73.

Earl, S., Carden, F., & Smutylo, T. (2001). *Outcome mapping: Building learning and reflection into development programs*. Ottawa: IDRC.

Evaluation Unit. (1992). *Evaluation strategy*. Ottawa: IDRC.

Evaluation Unit. (2009). *Capacity building at IDRC*. Retrieved from http://www.idrc.ca/evaluation_capacity

Evaluation Unit. (2010). *Evaluation unit report 2005–2010*. Ottawa: IDRC.

IDRC. (2000). *Program directions, 2000–2005*. Ottawa: Author.

IDRC. (2005). *Corporate strategy and program framework 2005–2010*. Ottawa: Author.

IDRC. (2006). A contemplative recess: IDRC's annual learning forum (ALF). *Evaluation Highlight #7*. Ottawa: Author.

IDRC. (2007). IDRC's approach to evaluation. *Evaluation highlight #12*. Ottawa: Author.

IDRC. (2010). *Innovating for development: Strategic framework 2010–2015.* Retrieved from http://www.idrc.ca/en/ev-149574–201–1-DO_TOPIC.html

Love, A. J. (2005). *External review of the IDRC evaluation unit.* Ottawa: IDRC.

Mintzberg, H. (2007). *Tracking strategies: Toward a general theory.* New York: Oxford University Press.

Patrizi, P., & Patton, M. Q. (2009). *Learning from doing: Reflections on IDRC's strategy in action.* Ottawa: IDRC.

Patton, M. Q. (2008). *Utilization-focused evaluation* (4th ed.). Thousand Oaks, CA: Sage.

Reychler, L., Sharbatke-Church, C., & Thomas, P. with Clegg, A., & Heilman, B. (2010). *External review of the Peace, Conflict and Development (PCD) Program.* Ottawa: IDRC.

Westley, F., Zimmerman, B., & Patton, M. Q. (2006). *Getting to maybe: How the world is changed.* Toronto: Random House.

TRICIA WIND *is senior program officer in the Evaluation Unit at the International Development Research Centre (Canada).*

FRED CARDEN *is the director of the Evaluation Unit at the International Development Research Centre (Canada).*

NEW DIRECTIONS FOR EVALUATION • DOI: 10.1002/ev

Patrizi, P. A. (2010). Death is certain, strategy isn't: Assessing the Robert Wood Johnson
Foundation's end-of-life grant making. In P. A. Patrizi & M. Q. Patton (Eds.), *Evaluating
strategy. New Directions for Evaluation, 128*, 47–68.

3

Death Is Certain, Strategy Isn't: Assessing the Robert Wood Johnson Foundation's End-of-Life Grant Making

Patricia A. Patrizi

Abstract

*The author discusses an assessment of the Robert Wood Johnson Foundation's
work over a 20-year period to improve end-of-life care in America. The case
illustrates the evolution of the strategy from one focused on a multiyear randomized control trial of a series of hospital-based interventions that produced
findings of "no effects" into several highly emergent approaches aiming to transform medical education and care delivery and launch a social movement to stimulate consumer and provider demand for better care. The case also illustrates
the challenges of discovering strategy in the absence of strategic plans. The
author illuminates the role a funder can play in shaping and executing strategic direction, facilitating and impeding progress in a field, and ultimately high-
lighting efforts made to build the field of end-of-life care. © Wiley Periodicals,
Inc., and the American Evaluation Association.*

Editors' Introduction

*T*his study began as a review of the Robert Wood Johnson Foundation's
grant making on end-of-life issues funded over a period of 20 years. It
was commissioned as a review of a diverse set of what turned out to be
more than 300 grants administered by different program officers under different

presidents focused on varying purposes. In doing the review the strategy became explicit and emerged as the thread that gave coherence to the diversity in the grant making. Independent of this review, the author was involved in surveying and interviewing participants of the Evaluation Roundtable about critical issues for evaluation. Evaluation of strategy emerged as a priority issue for both foundation evaluators and their chief executive officers. As a result of this emergent and unplanned convergence of interests around evaluating strategy, the review featured in the chapter was adapted and used as a teaching case in the Evaluation Roundtable. Publication of this case carries forward the commitment by the Evaluation Roundtable to make teaching cases widely accessible, as was done in an earlier volume of New Directions for Evaluation, *which explained teaching cases and offered three examples (Patrizi & Patton, 2005). This case adds to that collection.* MQP

Robert Wood Johnson Foundation Context

In 2006, the Robert Wood Johnson Foundation commissioned a strategic assessment of its investments to improve care at the end of life. The purpose was to create an overall learning opportunity for foundation staff and others interested in how foundations construct and execute grant-making strategies.

Having worked extensively with foundations attempting large-scale system change, we appreciated the degree of difficulty involved in this strategy. Improving care at the end of life implicated the Foundation in changing the medical establishment, including physicians, nursing, sites of care, the body of knowledge informing care at the end of life, as well as attempting to shape "demand for quality care" from those who were dying and their families. This also was to be accomplished in a relatively hostile context: The idea of "dying well" didn't have much currency with most families, who don't want their loved ones to die in the first place. Physicians are trained to cure and not necessarily to adopt what some see as the more passive position of offering "care." A wide range of incentives, including those driving the bottom line, motivates hospitals.

Therefore, we were acutely aware of how difficult it is to build a strong strategy focused on achieving sizeable and meaningful social impact from the platform of a foundation where staff must grapple with day-to-day dilemmas such as:

- Establishing achievable goals. Who or what target to change? How and where to intervene? What will it cost? Can anyone do the work? How much change is likely to occur? How much uncertainty is there about the problem and solutions? How much change is needed to make a significant difference?
- Setting strategy. How to know that progress is being made? When to stick with a strategy and when to alter direction and how to know one from the

NEW DIRECTIONS FOR EVALUATION • DOI: 10.1002/ev

other? What if the basic assumptions are wrong? What if the problem is far more complex than previously thought?

• Sustaining effects over time. How to ensure durability, if warranted, and/or proper adaptation? How to defend against unintended dissipation of effects postfunding? And is sustainability even possible or desirable?

These questions are vexing to most foundations engaging in social change. Nonetheless, struggling with these issues constitutes a bare-bones platform to consider whether or not a strategy is in place. When answered explicitly and openly, they can pave the way for productive focusing, efficient resource allocation, and greater realism, both within foundations and organizations in the fields they fund. But these questions are not answered easily or at one point in time. They are rarely, if ever, answered with certainty.

The Evaluation Charge and Its Challenges

The initial charge was to examine the strategy supporting grant making and to come to an assessment of the "whole effort" that occurred between 1996 and 2005—a 9-year period that came after an earlier significant investment in the same field. The original scope of the work focused on a sample of thirty grants selected by staff and considered most instrumental to achieving the program objectives:

1. To improve the knowledge and capacity of health care professionals and others to care for the dying.
2. To improve the institutional environment in health care institutions and in public policies and regulatory apparatus to enable better care of the dying.
3. To engage the public and professionals in efforts to improve end-of-life care (Weisfeld, Miller, Gibson, & Schroeder, 2000).

In the end the evaluation widened its aperture to encompass 337 grants and extended back over nearly 20 years, although we did not request additional funding for the evaluation. This important first lesson taught us that often small but pivotal efforts are ignored in favor of larger, more well-known efforts and that an early scan of the whole of the work is essential to understanding the strategy and its evolution.

Many other lessons surfaced during this evaluation that affected nearly every aspect of the evaluation design. For instance: What is strategy? For many, the word "strategy" has come to imply a formal set of steps: development of "theories of change" or "logic models," and identification and tracking of outputs and outcomes. These can be useful tools. But, for the most part, they did not exist in relation to this work. Also, we learned that strategy is rarely captured in documents and what was written often did a better job of expressing a vision than doing justice to the multitude of subtle ways that strategy was actually enacted. Nor did strategy documents begin to examine the *ways* through which behavior was to change. As a result, we had to draw inferences from what was done and what was said to uncover the parameters of what *might have been* the strategy.

Furthermore, we had to grapple with a range of theories about what constitutes good strategy. Because strategy is not an end in itself, we were confronted with the question—Is a strategy "good" if it is clearly articulated and measurable, as some would hold? Or is a strategy "good" when one that knows where it will land ahead of time, as some would hold? If these criteria were to be applied, we would have found the Robert Wood Johnson Foundation end-of-life strategy to be a failure, rather than the very successful effort we discovered it to be.

We knew that the retrospective nature of the work was particularly tricky. The evaluation was completed over 2 years and ultimately examined work reaching back to 1986, when the idea to invest in end-of-life issues first arose at the Foundation. Of those involved in the grant making, only two were still on the Foundation's staff, and many of the people we interviewed were challenged to reconstruct events from long ago. In considering how we would present this history, we tended to put more weight on impressions that could be corroborated by others or by documents. We also took care to see impressions as just that—impressionistic views on the climate and culture of decisions at the Foundation from years before. Ultimately, between 2006 and 2007, we interviewed 10 current and former RWJF staff, 31 grantees, and 32 nongrantees with knowledge of the Foundation's work in end-of-life care. Several of the main actors spoke to us on multiple occasions, and their remarks are cited here.

Also, we were acutely aware of changes in the way foundations now approach strategy development and execution as compared to then. We frequently found ourselves applying standards in this review that, with few exceptions, were not commonly appreciated in the field of philanthropy at the time. In some respects, this work adopts a more current view about strategy construction than was the case at the time of the grant making. We repeatedly took this into account and urge our readers to do so as well.

We learned a lot by looking at what was actually done—by looking at the grants—not just the "what" of the activities that were supported, but also the "who" and the "how" and what was learned in their own process. As we proceeded, we constructed straw-man strategies that we tested with staff in miniature bites, not wanting to seduce them or ourselves into a tidy package of retrospective rational order.

As we immersed ourselves in the work, we realized the interconnectedness of the efforts and came to understand that we needed a different lens to envision the strategy more clearly. We came to understand the most important lesson from this work: that strategy, particularly applied toward system change, must examine the underlying *dynamics of the system and the dynamics employed to foster change.*

NEW DIRECTIONS FOR EVALUATION • DOI: 10.1002/ev

Some of these dynamics include, but are not limited to:

- The nature of incentives that drive a system and influence and shape human behavior within it.
- How knowledge is used to stimulate action and foster adaptation when applied to regulate, set standards, motivate, etc.
- How problems are framed or reframed to enable action and break through logjams of indecision.
- The nature of communication, authority, and decision making over domains that might be considered emergent aspects of a "field."
- The "energy" of the field—the emotional content, which the end-of-life field surely has, but also the urgency and passion that was ignited and fueled over time to support individuals and groups to go beyond their day jobs—to take the steps, attend the meetings, resolve the conflict, and brainstorm the solutions that would ultimately lead to success.
- The relationships that constitute many of the flows within the system.
- Beyond networks, which were important, the strength of connections mattered a lot.

We also came to appreciate that beyond strategy we were watching the construction of an authentic field. The Foundation's investments in end-of-life work tell us much about the role a foundation plays in shaping and executing strategic direction, about how a foundation can both facilitate and impede progress in a field, and about how a foundation can take substantial steps to build that field by

- Identifying and framing an issue that captures public and professional emotion and attention.
- Coalescing ideas, knowledge, and professionals such that they can recognize each other as working within a burgeoning field.
- Helping key leaders grapple with strategic decisions.

Drawing a Circle Around What Constituted Strategy

A first important realization for the evaluation was that the strategy we were asked to evaluate—relating to grants made from 1996 through 2005—could not be done without considering the enormous impact of the Foundation's prior investment in understanding and responding to how Americans die.

From 1988 through 1994, the Robert Wood Johnson Foundation funded a landmark study of how Americans die, known as SUPPORT—Study to Understand Prognoses and Preferences for Outcomes and Risks of Treatments. SUPPORT gave credence to a growing, but until then unconfirmed, understanding of the shabby state of end-of-life care in this country.

For many in the health care field, the Foundation's investment in SUPPORT made the case that inadequacies of care at the end of life were profound, and that something could be done about it. The Foundation's investment in SUPPORT and its dissemination was considerable—$31 million over nearly 10 years. The returns were vast, although in unexpected ways.

SUPPORT sought first to understand the experience of those critically ill and dying in hospitals and then to test an intervention to address some of the significant shortfalls witnessed. Phase 1 was a descriptive, observational study of 4,301 patients hospitalized with life-threatening medical conditions, and expected to die within 6 months. During this phase, the researchers produced what for many was shocking information:

> Physicians did not know what patients wanted with regard to resuscitation. . .Orders against resuscitation were written in the last few days of life. Most patients who died in the hospital spent most of their last days on ventilators in intensive care. We had not expected to find the high levels of pain being reported, especially in non-cancer illnesses. Except for the comatose, more than half of the patients with any of the nine diseases were reported (by the patient or family member) to have substantial pain. (Lynn, 1997)

At the end of Phase 1, researchers concluded that physicians were unable to predict either severe disability or death and they had an inadequate understanding of their patients' wishes. Lewis Sandy, MD, who joined the Foundation some time later as Executive Vice President, understood the rationale for a second phase of SUPPORT as improving "prognosticating about death" and decisions that would be more in concert with the patient's wishes and trajectory.

> We needed to learn why patients were not getting the right care. We went after better and more detailed information that would allow us to know the likely trajectory of what would happen. We thought we would get the information and that should work to influence medical decisions. (L. Sandy, personal communication, May 2, 2007)

Convinced by expert consensus that targeted interventions would work, the research team "designed a second phase aimed at fixing these problems" (Schroeder, 1999). Phase 2 instituted a controlled clinical trial involving an experimental group of 2,652 seriously ill patients and a comparison group of similar size. Three interventions were offered:

- Validated prognostic models were developed for each patient so that physicians could estimate the likelihood of severe disability or death.
- Specially trained nurses talked with patients and their families to understand their wishes and to relay them to physicians and nurses involved.
- Detailed written instructions about patients and families' wishes regarding treatment were given to physicians.

NEW DIRECTIONS FOR EVALUATION • DOI: 10.1002/ev

SUPPORT Phase 2, implemented over 3 years, was expected to change the landscape of care in America. The Foundation was fully prepared for a large media push to publicize the positive results of SUPPORT. It was not to be. In 1994, researchers presented the totally unexpected and unequivocal finding of "no effects" to a stunned Foundation staff. In hindsight, many say that the SUPPORT strategy was overly "rational," and "underestimated the depth and complexity of the problem."

Understanding Strategy From the Perspective of Dynamics

Failure becomes an emotional call to action. The disappointing findings did not mark the end of the story. Steve Schroeder, then President of the Foundation, saw an opportunity to transform this great disappointment into a case for fundamental change. "I felt this was a chance to show that this was not a simple problem and that much needed to be done," he says. "This was a huge problem and we needed to put together a movement." Instead of the planned campaign to promote the success of SUPPORT, Schroeder and his communications staff refocused the campaign on the depth of the problem and the need to address it. The findings from SUPPORT made front-page news across the country (S. Schroeder, personal communication, May 7, 2007).

Many say that the Foundation's work to communicate the findings from SUPPORT was the real home run in the effort: Information from SUPPORT—and its credibility—galvanized professional awareness and action, unlike anything previous, around how Americans die.

Kathleen Foley, MD, Director of the Project on Death in America (PDIA), funded by the Open Society Institute, called publication of the SUPPORT study the "tipping point in the history of these movements and in public and professional discussions about end-of-life care, which validated widespread concerns among the public and health care professionals about the barriers and challenges to providing humane, compassionate care" (Foley, 2005). In fact, Foley credits the first SUPPORT study as part of the rationale for the Open Society Institute's investment in PDIA.

According to Foley, a consensus about care at the end of life emerged from this work: the problem was serious and complex and "significant barriers—organizational, institutional, educational, and economic—had to be overcome before end-of-life care could be improved" (Foley, 2005, and personal communication, January 16, 2006).

The Climate for Strategy

Much debate and several landmark events shaped the Foundation's work in this area. In the early 1990s, the nation was immersed in a struggle about care at the end of life. New laws and high-profile court cases made headlines. Jack Kevorkian, or "Dr. Death" as he was known, came to public attention with his first known assisted suicide. The Patient Self-Determination Act

NEW DIRECTIONS FOR EVALUATION • DOI: 10.1002/ev

came into law and required hospitals to inform patients of their right to make treatment choices regarding resuscitation and other lifesaving technology. In 1994, Oregon residents voted to approve the Death with Dignity Act to legalize euthanasia. At the same time, health experts and the public pondered the implications of shifts in demography, epidemiology, and biomedical technology. What were the moral, medical, and economic principles that should guide our choices? Although Medicare provided benefits for hospice care, relatively few people took advantage of them. Only a small proportion of Americans had advance directives to guide their care. In this context, the Robert Wood Johnson Foundation entered the end-of-life care field, anew.

After SUPPORT ended in 1994, the Foundation was uncertain about how to move forward and began what one Foundation executive called "a collective head scratch." Unsure about what would work and wanting to address "a broad array of factors leading to social change," staff sought to "activate an impassioned consumer movement" that would motivate the public and professionals and help transform the culture of institutions charged with delivering care to the critically ill (Weisfeld, Miller, Gibson, & Schroeder, 2000).

Over the next year, a staff team was formed to address issues related to care at the end of life. A communications team was already in gear from its work on SUPPORT. An Institute of Medicine (IOM) report, "Approaching Death: Improving Care at the End of Life" (Field & Cassel, 1997), partially funded by RWJF, came to frame the clinical and related system issues for the field and became an important source document for the Foundation. It was not until some time in 1997 that the Foundation formalized its objectives for moving forward.

Learning While Doing: Promoting Excellence

Promoting Excellence was launched 1 year after the grant to the IOM and 2 years after SUPPORT findings were released. With the passage of time, staff recognized that "something needed to be done but there was no scalable response quite in sight as yet" (R. Gibson, personal communication, June 5, 2006).

Promoting Excellence was in many ways a direct reaction to what many called the overdose of confidence built into the assumption behind SUPPORT—that the problem was well understood and that solutions were fairly clear. After the SUPPORT evaluation indicated otherwise, Promoting Excellence was cast as a search for "models that work."

Promoting Excellence aimed to demonstrate that palliative care services could be delivered in many different settings and to people with vastly different conditions. The program portfolio was highly varied, serving special populations including children, prisoners, Native Americans, the seriously mentally ill, urban African Americans, and others. It also focused on special conditions and diseases including Alzheimer's, HIV/AIDS, and advanced renal, liver, lung, heart, and kidney disease. The projects were located in difficult settings, including cancer centers, nursing homes, prisons, mental institutions, and group homes, as well as hard-to-serve rural and urban communities. Although all but 2 of the 26 projects continued in some form, few patient-outcome reports were collected or assessed. The projects, however, produced volumes of articles addressing operational and clinical care issues.

Recognizing and Capitalizing Upon Opportunity

Ira Byock, MD, Director of the Promoting Excellence National Program Office, described often as a "passionate advocate" and "visionary," was an emergency medicine physician who understood the importance of translating the need for and practice of palliative care to physicians who were most on the line to save or extend life. (For a description of most Robert Wood Johnson Foundation end-of-life programs, see grant results reports available at www.rwjf.org.)

After receiving 678 letters of intent responding to the call for proposals, Byock saw an opportunity to work with medical specialties and their leaders. These "thought leaders" were convened over 2 years into eight Peer Workgroups focused primarily on specific diseases or conditions, thereby building a network of more than 200 mainstream specialists. The Peer Workgroups emerged as an unanticipated success in developing palliative care strongholds within specialty areas—generally not the most fertile ground for palliative care. As one observer said, "The impact of the work groups was breathtaking. The surgery and critical care groups were incredible at digging in. They looked at the quality domains that were at the core of the discipline of palliative care and said, 'We have to integrate this'" (I. Byock, personal communication, February 7, 2007).

The Promoting Excellence national program office used the program to make the case for "the larger do-ability" of palliative care—one that could be acceptable to a broad range of clinicians and people and successfully administered earlier in an illness than most had previously assumed possible. Byock, reflecting back on the start of the grants, said, "Nine years ago, there were serious questions about whether it was even possible to provide palliative care at the same time clinicians are actively treating cancer or heart problems. The projects demonstrated that you can provide concurrent palliative care without requiring patients to give up active, disease modifying treatment."

Reforming the Delivery of Care: Two Theories

Staff believed that to change care in meaningful ways they needed to change physicians, and how they are educated, as the primary priority. Referring to hospice and palliative-care–related education, two of the field's early leaders wrote: "These programs won't produce real change unless they also address the hidden curriculum of medical schools—the values, attitudes and beliefs that constitute the basic culture of medicine" (Sullivan, Lakoma, & Block, 2003). With this in mind, Foundation staff sought to focus its attention on medicine and nursing and employed two very different theories of change.

To reach practicing physicians, RWJF funded the American Medical Association through Education in Palliative and End-of-Life Care (EPEC) to develop curriculum and implement a train-the-trainer model that theoretically would reach *all* practicing physicians in the United States relying on an ever-growing pyramid of successive retraining. EPEC developed and implemented training with a nine-module training curriculum.

An evaluation conducted in 2003 (Sutton Group) found that EPEC was most likely to reach health care providers already interested in palliative care, rather than those who were resistant or disinterested. They concluded that targeting "all physicians" did little to help the program develop strategies to address differences within its target audience adequately. In all likelihood, change in each of these groups would have called for different strategies (if, in fact, change could have been achieved at all with some segments).

The evaluation also produced information questioning the assumption that physicians would have time available in their schedules to devote to training. As it turned out training was delivered largely to allied health professionals rather than the doctors themselves. More than 50% of the trainers surveyed indicated that less than one-third of those they trained were physicians.

Despite these flawed assumptions, there were significant achievements. By all accounts, the program succeeded in developing a core curriculum for palliative care that has been adapted and adopted by many others. The substantive material produced has served to inform education standards and has populated much of the substance in educational programs for the VA health system, osteopaths, and specialty areas and has been replicated and modified for many specialty groups, including emergency medicine, geriatrics, and oncology.

Systems Reform: Understanding the Dynamics of Systems and System Leverage

The core theory of change underlying medical education reform centered on stimulating demand for palliative care knowledge and practitioners by changing the licensing tests administered to physicians at three different times in their educational career. The same approach was adopted with some modifications by nursing as well.

The strategy was jointly constructed by Foundation staff with key leaders in the field, particularly Foley of PDIA. It was based on the following theory and system dynamics of how medical education works:

- Institutions need external motivation to change.
- Changes in the medical licensing exam would provide an incentive to teach to the test.

NEW DIRECTIONS FOR EVALUATION • DOI: 10.1002/ev

- Changes in the exam would require new knowledge.
- New knowledge would require researchers to produce it, a curriculum to organize it and faculty trained to teach it.

Key to all of this work was a small 1998 grant awarded to the National Board of Medical Examiners to strengthen end-of-life content in medical licensing exams. Students and later physicians take these exams at the end of the second year of medical school on basic sciences, at the end of the fourth year on clinical sciences, and finally after one or more postgraduate years in preparation for acquiring a medical license.

In line with the plan to build incentives, the Foundation also made a series of targeted grants that would help meet the demand for knowledge created by the test, including supporting an audit of textbook content that publishers responded to resoundingly; curriculum and training of residency program directors in end-of-life material (as of 2006, 347 programs had completed the training); similar effort for medical schools; and establishing a Web-based resource center with peer-reviewed educational materials, recommended books and articles, training opportunities, funding sources, conferences, and links to resources.

The Foundation also made a grant to the Veterans Administration as a relatively quick way to have a large impact. Overall, the VA offers approximately 15% of the fellowship slots in palliative care in the United States. By 2003, the VA issued formal standards for palliative care and mandated that all units have palliative care services.

One of the most influential factors in shaping the Foundation's approach to reforming medical education was the relationship that developed between Kathleen Foley and Rosemary Gibson, one of the lead program officers at RWJF. PDIA's most significant program, The Faculty Scholars Program, was to become the most important source of leadership for the Robert Wood Johnson Foundation's emerging program.

A key decision, which put this partnership to the test, emerged around the question of whether palliative care needed to become a subspecialty. It provides an excellent illustration of how two organizations, PDIA and RWJF, could work in a genuine and sustained partnership building on complementary roles and perspectives.

PDIA and RWJF were not fully on the same page regarding the need for specialists in palliative care. RWJF did not want "to add to medical divisiveness and fragmentation," so abstained from taking a position, choosing to "let physicians do this themselves," and to respond to requests from the field (R. Gibson, personal communication, March 12, 2007).

PDIA, on the other hand, wholly endorsed the creation of a subspecialty that could assume status and position within medicine. PDIA's Foley believed in the importance of following an "elite strategy." As she saw it, "The only way to address the issue was to create a subspecialty informed by a clear and well-respected base of knowledge. These specialists would be charged to create curriculum and teach. But to be taken seriously, they would need the same credentials and quality of knowledge that their colleagues commanded; from this would follow the demand for and earned respect" (Foley, 2005, and personal communication, January 16, 2006).

In straddling this issue, RWJF supported the American Board of Hospice and Palliative Medicine (ABHPM) to take the necessary steps to build the accreditation process for fellowship training programs, improve the certification exam for physicians in the field, and adopt a plan for a recertification test.

PDIA provided support to ABHPM to take a leadership role in formalizing recognition of hospice and palliative medicine—the more politicized position. With this combined support, ABHPM helped hospice and palliative medicine achieve recognition as a medical subspecialty in near-record time. In 2006, the American Board of Medical Specialties agreed to recognize hospice and palliative medicine as a legitimate subspecialty, and the Accreditation Council for Graduate Medical Education voted to accredit fellowship training programs.

Reforming Nursing Education

The rationale and strategy for nursing paralleled the approach employed in medical education reform. As with medicine, the nursing approach was grounded in research illustrating that nurses were inadequately prepared to care for patients in pain or at the end of life. The goal was to address this deficiency by embedding end-of-life care content into nursing textbooks, teaching, licensure, and certification.

Like medicine, the nursing education reform efforts applied a "push strategy": If new licensing and certification procedures required knowledge and skills in end-of-life care, then these requirements would drive demand for nursing textbooks, curricula, and training programs with the necessary content.

In 1997, RWJF supported the American Academy of Colleges for Nursing (AACN) to convene a roundtable of nurse educators, clinicians, and researchers. The result was *A Peaceful Death: Recommended Competencies and Curriculum Guidelines for End-of-Life Care*. These competencies were made part of the baccalaureate essentials of nursing education. Also, they provided the framework for the End-of-Life Care Nursing Education Consortium (ELNEC) training program established three years later with RWJF support to design and use an evidence-based curriculum to train undergraduate nursing faculty and continuing education providers and to incorporate what they learned into their home institutions.

Investments in improving nursing came about through dogged advocacy by a handful of nursing leaders who "knew what needed to be done." It was a well-designed strategy that was effectively executed, with documented effects. Reflecting on the work, Foundation staff say "they knew nursing would get it right and do it meticulously" (R. Gibson, personal communication, June 5, 2006). The partnership with AACN was the essential instrument. As a membership organization of more than 800 schools of nursing, it could engage nursing colleges effectively and bring credibility to the ELNEC training.

The nurses made significant strides in building their part of the field:

- Palliative care competencies added to the essentials of baccalaureate nursing education.
- Forty percent of authors and publishers made changes to major nursing textbooks after a content audit revealed that only 2% had any relevant material on end of life.
- The National Council of State Boards of Nursing revised their test plan to include improved end-of-life content in the exam for registered nurses.
- The Hospice and Palliative Nurses Association (formerly Hospice Nurses Association) started in 1987 and as of 2008 had over 9,200 members (http://www.hpna.org).
- Within 1 year of ELNEC training, 500 nurse faculty had trained 19,000 students. As of 2004, 1,400 nurse educators were trained, representing at the time, one-third of nursing schools in all 50 states.

Understanding the Linkages Among Research, Education, Training, and Care Delivery

The Center to Advance Palliative Care (CAPC) originally came about as a way to provide teaching demonstration sites for residency training. CAPC became the lynchpin in the education and care delivery system developed by the Foundation in concert with PDIA and other leaders in the field. For this "push" of the medical education system to work fully, students would need clinical sites to observe and practice, and these sites—namely, hospitals—would need incentives to use the knowledge. Other advantages to the strategy include:

- Research conducted within palliative care centers translates into knowledge and practices used in training physicians.
- Employment opportunities are developed for fellows or others with training in palliative care.
- Centers are located in the heart of the health care system and help build the demand for palliative care expertise within it.

While viewed modestly in the beginning, this line of grant making evolved to become a significant part of the portfolio and the main way to promote and anchor palliative care in hospitals.

The Center's first grant, awarded in 1999, established a National Resource Center for Palliative Care at Mount Sinai School of Medicine in New York. The grant's aims were to:

- Increase the number of hospitals with capability to provide quality palliative care.

- Create sufficient momentum that hospital-based palliative care becomes standard practice in comprehensive patient care.
- Provide leadership in the development of standards for palliative care programs.

In 2000, 632 hospitals had palliative care capability. RWJF hoped to increase this to 20% of the hospitals in the United States. To support this goal the foundation supported the Joint Commission[1] to develop and implement standards regarding palliative care practices.

Why Hospitals?

An important question addressed in this assessment was: Why hospitals? They are complex institutions, under financial duress, and not likely candidates to think differently about palliative care. Why not consider nursing homes, as they serve predominantly the very old? Why not address the severe shortages in community-based care? Or why not deal with what many considered the root of the problem—the inadequacies in the role of primary care for those in need of palliative services?

The logic offered by Foundation staff and confirmed by many observers was that the hospital-based strategy made sense for the following reasons, some of which include:

- The hospital is the site where most people die.
- The costs associated with the end of life are staggering and most are incurred in the hospital.
- Hospitals have incentives to address these issues to cut costs, as outlier patients with palliative care needs can absorb enormous resources.

Staff also recognized that significant strategic barriers make alternatives difficult to pursue, including:

- The inadequacy of the primary care system in America.
- No viable community health system that can adequately provide palliative care.
- Insufficient prospective reimbursement for home health to cover good palliative care, and weak system of delivery.
- Nursing homes do not have the level, quantity, and stability of professional staff that would foster a system of palliative care.
- Hospices, while addressing care needs of the dying, do not represent the mainstream of medicine or a major component of the health care system.

Diane Meier, MD, CAPC's director, would be among the first to say that the hospital palliative care center cannot transform the entire system of care for the seriously ill. Nevertheless, in the current U.S. health care system where hospitals and medical centers dominate the marketplace, they were seen as the most pragmatic and cost-effective means to improve existing care rapidly, and as a base upon which other palliative care interventions could be constructed across the continuum of care.

Addressing Demand Pressures

The demand for CAPC's services quickly increased beyond the ability of the Center. In part, growth resulted from the success of other elements of the Foundation's grant making. As part of the Foundation's communications campaign they supported a number of important and influential television projects. One of these, Bill Moyers' program, *On Our Own Terms*,[2] featured CAPC, which in turn received more than 1,200 requests from hospitals asking for information and help.

To help CAPC respond to this growing interest, in 2003, the Foundation funded CAPC to establish Palliative Care Leadership Centers (PCLCs) to train six PCLCs to help hospitals and hospices establish and sustain palliative care programs. The goals included building a cadre of leaders, strengthening exemplary programs, and developing working relationships so that CAPC and the PCLCs could aggregate their data and move quickly to support change. CAPC has developed a large body of "how to" materials and provides technical assistance related to operating palliative care centers in hospitals successfully.

Reframing the Issue From End of Life to Palliative Care

Diane Meier, MD, understood that she had to "sell" palliative care and brought in marketing, business modeling, and financial expertise to do so.

Important early marketing decisions helped position CAPC not as a traditional advocacy organization, but as one with great technical skills and a strong product to sell. Early on, Meier worked with Sutton Group,[3] a social marketing firm, to develop a segmented market analysis of her audience, building upon a data-based analysis of who the audiences are, what they want, and the factors that influence their choices. With Sutton, she identified six important but very different audiences for palliative care centers and concluded that they had very different needs—the audiences ranged from patients and their families to doctors with very different perspectives on how to treat those who are terminally ill. Also included were hospital CEOs, whose needs had not previously been factored in by advocates in this area. On this point, Meier remarked: Palliative care physicians often view CEOs as the enemy. We teach that "you're on the same side of the table as the hospital CEO. If the CEO can't keep the hospital doors open, your service will close. You can help your CEO assure high quality care, through-put and highly technical efficiency. If you look at payment by diagnosis for a hospital stay—if you have someone with a sixty-day length of stay, that's blocking

23 admissions and that's a huge loss to the hospital. It happens that palliative care improves operations" (D. Meier, personal communication, March 16, 2007).

Rather than arguing for the innate social good of the CAPC product, Meier came to an assessment of her market that ran against the conventional wisdom espoused by most of her colleagues, who tended to believe that *all physicians should* incorporate palliative care into their medical practices. Instead, she saw palliative care specialists as stepping up to support admitting physicians when they needed assistance. She understood that she needed to demonstrate that palliative care made financial sense for hospitals and built and disseminated business case models.

Most importantly, she worked to reframe the problem and goal from offering care toward a "good death" to providing care to those who are seriously ill in hospitals. This approach expanded both the target population and the acceptability of the services of these centers. The work was not without challenges for Meier. Meier had to "come to terms with the limited market for good dying." She concluded that "the notion that a very sick person is interested in a good death is wrong. We get feedback from our palliative care website saying, 'I clicked on your resources, but my dad doesn't need hospice. He's not dying.' Phrases like 'good care of the dying' or 'bereavement' turn people off."

But the payoff has been noteworthy. CAPC is as well regarded by CEOs as it is by clinicians and advocates for care of this kind. The outcomes have been significant: nationally, 53% of all U.S. hospitals with 50+ beds, and 75% of hospitals with 300+ beds, have adopted palliative care programs (Morrison, Dietrich, & Meier, 2008). The program trained 572 hospital teams and 88% of them started palliative care programs within 2 years. CAPC also has had a central role along with the American Academy of Hospice and Palliative Care, Hospice and Palliative Nurses Association, Last Acts Partnership, and National Hospice and Palliative Care Organization in developing the National Consensus Project (NCP) Guidelines for Quality Palliative Care. In turn, these guidelines became the basis for the National Quality Forum framework for palliative and hospice care, which many consider to be the first step in receiving direct Medicare reimbursement.

Building a Policy Infrastructure: Several Approaches

Although policy was woven throughout much of the work described above, several other important efforts took shape with RWJF's support: policies affecting pain management and adding to the field's capacity to measure and regulate quality. The Foundation funded two grantees at the University of Wisconsin: David Joranson, MSW, director of the Pain and Policy Studies Group, and June Dahl, Professor of Pharmacology in the medical school. Dahl worked with The Joint Commission to integrate pain assessment and management into the standards used to accredit health care facilities across the United States. The standards primarily affect hospitals, but long-term care and home health programs are increasingly seeking Joint Commission accreditation.

Long an advocate of sound pain policies, Joranson's work focused on improving policy at the state level, establishing the first state Cancer Pain Initiative in Wisconsin, then emulated by 46 other states. Joranson had received grants from RWJF going back to the mid-1980s. His work produced one of the most effective devices in the portfolio to create state change. From 2000 through 2007, his state pain policy progress report cards graded states on the quality of pain policies and regulations, and were an important catalyst toward changing state policies and regulations. From 2000 to 2003 alone, 16 states increased their report card grade (Pain & Policy Studies Group, 2003). From 2003 to 2006, 19 states improved at least one grade level (Gilson, Joranson, & Maurer, 2007). The report cards then were supported by the American Cancer Society, the Susan G. Komen Foundation for the Cure, and the Lance Armstrong Foundation.

As early as 1992, Dahl received RWJF support to develop a network of State Pain Initiatives to overcome barriers to pain relief. In 1996, a national organization, the Alliance of State Pain Initiatives, was established. With Joranson, Dahl worked with the federal Drug Enforcement Agency (DEA) to develop a statement calling for a balance between addressing abuse and diversion of prescription pain medicines and maintaining access for patients. As a result of this collaboration, the DEA issued a joint statement in 2001 with a coalition of health care and pain prevention organizations calling for a more balanced opioid medication policy. Unfortunately, the dialogue between the DEA and pain community came to a halt a few years after this statement, as the DEA appeared to pull back from its earlier commitment (Duensing, 2006).

Along with Joranson and Dahl, the Community-State Partnerships to Improve Care at the End of Life funded coalitions in 23 states, in part, to advocate for policy change. Several of the Community-State Partnerships, particularly those that included the state pain initiatives as coalition partners, worked closely with Dahl and Joranson to promote the pain report card and advocate for state policy change. These partnerships addressed many other issues as well. Some of the most effective dealt with advance directives, Medicaid reimbursement, and nursing home quality.

Much excellent work addressed both the undertreatment of pain and striking a better balance between regulators' concerns about diversion and abuse of controlled substances and physicians' ability to prescribe medication for pain management without fear of undue scrutiny. With the recent prosecution of some physicians for their prescribing practices, and the lack of clarity about the moral rectitude of administering medication to those in pain, there seems to be significant risk that ground will be lost.

On the issue of quality, Joan Teno, MD, Associate Director of Brown University Medical School's Center for Gerontology and Health Care Research, received Foundation support for over a decade to create and test new instruments to measure institutional care at the end of life and develop a Web interface where health care providers can download instruments, submit data, and get results back evaluating their quality of care. Her work has made an important mark. In 2004, the National Hospice and Palliative Care Organization (NHPCO), which represents 80% of hospices nationwide, took over and adapted much of Teno's toolkit. The group now analyzes the data for its members.

In addition, Teno received a grant to disseminate national, state, and local indicators of change in end-of-life care. The resulting *Facts on Dying* Web site contains policy-relevant information, including trends in site of death, family perceptions of end-of-life care as well as other important indicators, such as the presence of pain, advance directives, do-not-resuscitate orders, and feeding tubes for nursing home residents and the severely cognitively impaired.

Many of those interviewed credit Teno for significant advances in the field. Said one: "There has been tremendous uptake of her work in quality. I can honestly say that Teno has redefined how we think about quality related to palliative care and has been instrumental in thinking about quality from the patient and family's perspective."

Building Public and Professional Will

Communications played a central role in the end-of-life portfolio from the outset and throughout. The Foundation's communication staff was well into developing a media campaign to promote the results from the SUPPORT study even before the results were known. Perhaps for this reason, the Foundation's communications grant making was first out the door among the overall end-of-life care portfolio and is credited with helping to put SUPPORT into the public and professional consciousness.

Once it became clear that SUPPORT was not effective in changing how people were dying, the Foundation staff decided to transform their great disappointment into work on a campaign to highlight the depth of the problem and issue a call to action to the health care community and the public at large. The resulting Foundation-coordinated press campaign helped to get SUPPORT findings covered in a front-page story in the *Boston Globe* and on the *ABC Nightly News* with Peter Jennings. This attention was important, galvanizing many actors in the health care system.

In 1995, the Foundation funded Last Acts, its first program after the release of SUPPORT findings, even before it developed the end-of-life care portfolio's three objectives. Last Acts was "a coalition of professional and consumer organizations dedicated to making the public more aware of end-of-life issues and finding better ways to care for the dying." Its charge was to "work through [national] organizations and the media" to promote end-of-life issues. Specific activities included producing a Web site, a quarterly print newsletter, a weekly e-mail newsletter, a bimonthly partner memo, and various media relations activities to promote end-of-life issues geared to public as well as policymaker audiences.

Last Acts was perhaps most influenced by Schroeder's call for a "broad social movement." At one point it had over 48 objectives and four goals in its effort to respond to the large set of issues emerging from communities.

As noted earlier, the Foundation also invested in several other efforts to motivate and/or educate the public directly. The most prominent of these was support of *On Our Own Terms*, a four-part public television series by journalist Bill Moyers. At the time of its airing, this important series was viewed by more Americans than any other program in public television history. Other noteworthy programming included support for *Wit*, an HBO adaptation of the play about a doctor diagnosed with cancer and grappling with the indignities of the disease and the health care system, as well as a documentary on Dame Cicely Saunders, founder of the hospice movement. These and other efforts aimed to portray end-of-life decisions quite differently from what the public had seen before.

Strategy Observations

SUPPORT remains the single most important source of knowledge in the area. No study before or since has looked so closely and systematically at how people die in America. Its approach was rigorous and its researchers beyond reproach; the study's credibility was never an issue. The Foundation is to be credited for seeing this as an important moment to make a clarion call to action. It succeeded in mobilizing parts of the medical community and, more importantly, in moving the issue from the fringe to the center of the health care debate.

Buoyed by this new environment, a group of leaders in the field used Foundation support and accomplished significant advances, including:

1. Created demand for enhanced knowledge and skills in end-of-life care by identifying and pushing key levers within the medical and nursing education systems. By engaging and convincing the National Board of Medical Examiners and National Council of State Boards of Nursing to include questions on palliative care in their licensing exams for physicians and nurses, grantees were able to set off the creation of a series of incentives which went far to align the rest of the system.
2. Enabled The Joint Commission to develop a new standard for assessment and treatment and of pain.
3. Created a supply of knowledge to meet new demand by supporting research, publishing, curricula development, and approaches to training faculty.
4. Created an institutional driver, the Center to Advance Palliative Care at Mount Sinai School of Medicine in New York, to meet increased demand for knowledge of palliative care within the hospital setting, and

New Directions for Evaluation • DOI: 10.1002/ev

did it in a way that was acceptable to hospital CEOs, admitting physicians and specialists alike.

5. Supported some of the core infrastructure needs of an emerging field by developing standards of care and the capacity to assess and monitor those standards across institutional settings.

6. Brought attention to the quality of pain treatment in states with regulatory policies that inhibit physicians in caring properly for patients in pain.

7. Fostered, in partnership with the Project on Death in America, the advancement of careers and emerging leadership in a relatively undeveloped field.

8. Created an enormous base of knowledge in a relatively short period of time, particularly in areas of clinical care and organization and delivery of services.

9. Between 1996 and 2006, more than 2,800 physicians obtained certification from the American Board of Hospice and Palliative Medicine.

10. In 1988, the American Academy of Hospice and Palliative Medicine began with 250 founding members; in 2008, it had more than 2,600 members (AAHPM Web site, Kuehn, 2007).

The Foundation clearly had the wherewithal and fortitude to pursue an important issue at a moment when it occupied the attention of the public in dramatic ways. Yet it was more than just good timing. Foundation staff played a critical role in making these advances possible, and they did so with more than just the provision of funds.

Staff were in the mix with leaders of the field, in essence, helping to shape and frame an agenda for action based on the best kind of insider knowledge of how a system works, straddling the boundary of inside and outside the field. This role is important, and it was done well.

The resulting strategy, therefore, was informed and subtle enough to identify real and powerful incentives and leverage points that could magnify small actions into far larger-than-expected effects. The intelligence of this work came from a deep understanding of real relationships and how the broader system of medicine actually works.

The strategy identified a few key leverage points, chosen because they had power to entrain other subsequent actions and effects. If achieved, the goals—like changes in licensing—would set off ripple effects throughout the system. To some extent, this systems approach obviated the need to worry about "institutionalizing" the Foundation's work. As the work was being done, it was built into existing structures and positions. For the most part, new organizations were not created; rather, existing organizations were given incentives to align with the goals of the effort, thereby mitigating issues of sustainability. Grantees were often chosen because of their credibility and power to influence key decision makers.

The strategy also considered where change was most likely to occur, and weighed the potential investments based on their relative risks. Where strong players were not in place and opportunities to advance change less likely, investments were not made.

We don't want to exaggerate the positive outcomes of the work—either how it was done or the consequences of some of the decisions made.

- It evolved and got better over time. There were some weak choices, particularly early on, but staff learned from them and applied the lessons.
- To some extent, the best work was happenstance. But when good work was occurring, the officers recognized it and made the most out of it.
- Staff had high standards for identifying good work and good people and kept a relentless eye on discerning whether and what kind of change was achievable.
- The strength of the work came from the strength of ties to the field.
- When high-leverage projects were identified, the officer supported them well, and consequently said no or delayed response to many others.
- Some of its success relates to the time span covered: over 20 years—a relative eon in today's terms.

Conclusions

The grant making under end of life was extraordinary in many ways, and the results are tangible. The work helped produce a body of knowledge, leading practitioners, standards for practice, ways to assess quality, and changes in how pain is assessed and treated. Without a doubt, palliative care now has a meaning within medicine and its institutions that didn't exist before. There was significant systems change as a direct result of Foundation grants. And there was individual change: Many more people now have advance directives, and, in most states, they are becoming more enforceable. The Foundation, without question, helped build a field.

This story holds broader implications for foundation strategy across the sector. The Foundation's investments in end of life tell us much about the role of a foundation—what it can do, what influence it can exert, how it can shape an agenda, and how it can both facilitate and impede a field. We suspect, but will never know for sure, that more could have been done if the Foundation had forged a deeper alliance among the parts of the whole.

Still, the Robert Wood Johnson Foundation advanced a field rich with talent and ideas—not through luck (or luck alone), but through strategy. It was not the kind of strategy based on the inputs, outputs, and outcomes derived from "logic models," but strategy built on close-to-the-ground reconnaissance, intimate understanding of how systems work and develop, and, most important, a deep appreciation of and willingness to work side by side with talent in the field.

Notes

1. The Joint Commission is the nation's oldest and largest standards setting and accrediting body in health care. Throughout this document, we refer to The Joint Commission, which had been called the Joint Commission on Accreditation of Health Care Organizations (JCAHO) during the period from 1987 through 2006.
2. In September 2000, the Public Broadcasting Service (PBS) aired "On Our Own Terms: Moyers on Dying." Bill Moyers and the Educational Broadcasting Corporation produced the series, which explored different aspects of dying and drew 16 million viewers.
3. Sutton Group had just completed a study of EPEC and applied this knowledge of physician preferences to their work with CAPC.

References

Duensing, L. (2006). Talking with June Dahl, Ph.D.: The impact of legislative and regulatory policy on the practice of pain management in the United States. *The Pain Practitioner, 16*(4), 27–30.

Field, M., & Cassel, C.K. (1997). *Approaching death, improving care at the end of life.* Washington, DC: Committee on Care at the End of Life, Division of Health Care Services, Institute of Medicine, National Academies Press.

Foley, K. M. (2005, November/December). The past and future of palliative care. *Hastings Center Report, S*, 42–56.

Gilson, A., Joranson, D., & Maurer, A. (2007). Improving state pain policies: Recent progress and continuing opportunities. *CA: A Cancer Journal for Clinicians, 57*, 341–353.

Kuehn, B. (2007). Hospitals embrace palliative care. *Medical News & Perspectives, 298*(11), 1263–1265.

Lynn, J. (1997). Unexpected returns, insights from SUPPORT. In S. L. Isaacs & J. R. Knickman (Eds.), *To improve health and health care* (Vol. 1). Princeton, NJ: The Robert Wood Johnson Foundation.

Morrison, S., Dietrich, J., & Meier, D. (2008). *America's care of serious illness: A state-by-state report card on access to palliative care in our nation's hospitals.* New York: Center to Advance Palliative Care.

Pain & Policy Studies Group. (2003). *Achieving balance in state pain policy: A progress report card.* Madison: University of Wisconsin Comprehensive Cancer Center.

Patrizi, P., & Patton, M. Q. (Eds.). (2005). *Teaching evaluation using the case method. New Directions for Evaluation,* 105.

Schroeder, S. A. (1999). The legacy of SUPPORT. *Annals of Internal Medicine, 131*, 780–782.

Sullivan, A. M., Lakoma, M. D., & Block, S. D. (2003). The status of medical education in end-of-life-care. *Journal of General Internal Medicine, 18*, 684–695.

Sutton Group. (2000). *EPEC marketing research, topline findings.* Microsoft PowerPoint presentation. Washington, DC: Sutton Group.

Weisfeld, V., Miller, D., Gibson, R., & Schroeder, S. A. (2000). Improving care at the end of life: What does it take?" *Health Affairs, 19*(6), 277–283.

PATRICIA A. PATRIZI *is chair of the Evaluation Roundtable and principal of Patrizi Associates, Philadelphia.*

Sherwood, K. E. (2010). The W. K. Kellogg Foundation's Devolution Initiative: An experiment in evaluating strategy. In P. A. Patrizi & M. Q. Patton (Eds.), *Evaluating strategy. New Directions for Evaluation, 128,* 69–86.

4

The W. K. Kellogg Foundation's Devolution Initiative: An Experiment in Evaluating Strategy

Kay E. Sherwood

Abstract

When Congress passed and President Bill Clinton signed a major welfare reform law in 1996, there were significant concerns across the public policy spectrum about how it would be implemented and how it would affect poor families, in part because the law shifted much responsibility for decision making from the federal government to state and local officials, a process called "devolution." The Kellogg Foundation was one of the concerned parties, and, as a result, it launched the Devolution Initiative to learn about the changes taking place and mobilize responses to the reform as its implications unfolded. The author revisits the Foundation's Devolution Initiative and its external evaluation from the perspective of evaluation as a strategic intervention. © Wiley Periodicals, Inc., and the American Evaluation Association.

The original research for this chapter was aided by interviews with more than a dozen W. K. Kellogg Foundation staff, and the Devolution Initiative (DI) evaluators, to whom the author is grateful for their time, their thoughtfulness, and their candor about the challenges of an unprecedented intervention. I particularly thank Alice Warner-Mehlhorn and Diane Smith at the Foundation, who provided access to the historical records and the historical memory of the DI, and to Teresa Behrens, the former director of evaluation at the Foundation, who facilitated the process of telling the DI story and provided critical insights.

Editors' Introduction

*S*trategy unfolds at multiple levels and in multiple arenas. This case looks at the intersections and interplays among a U.S. federal government strategic policy, a major philanthropic foundation strategic initiative designed to influence the federal strategy, and an evaluation strategy focused on influencing and assessing the foundation strategy. It is the story of the W. K. Kellogg Foundation's (WKKF) Devolution Initiative (DI). Figure 4.1 depicts the strategic interrelationships that unfold in this case study.

This case was originally written as an evaluation teaching case for the Evaluation Roundtable, which has as its purpose the development of a community of practice among evaluation professionals working in philanthropy. We previously edited a volume of New Directions for Evaluation with teaching cases developed for the Evaluation Roundtable (Patrizi & Patton, 2005) and Kay Sherwood, the author of this case, wrote two of those earlier teaching cases (Sherwood, 2005a, 2005b). As we planned this volume, we thought it would be instructive to revisit the devolution story told here through the lens of strategy to illuminate issues of evaluating strategy at the different levels and in these varying but interrelated arenas as depicted in Exhibit 1 of the Patton and Patrizi article (this issue). The lens of evaluating strategy is being applied retrospectively, because that was not how those involved framed the issues at the time. Had the framework of evaluating strategy been available and used at the time, it might have clarified important issues and made key tensions more manageable. Readers can judge for themselves whether this is the case. Most of this case study focuses on what the strategies were in each arena, how they intersected, and the implications for evaluation.

Figure 4.1. Interrelated Strategic Arenas in the Devolution Case

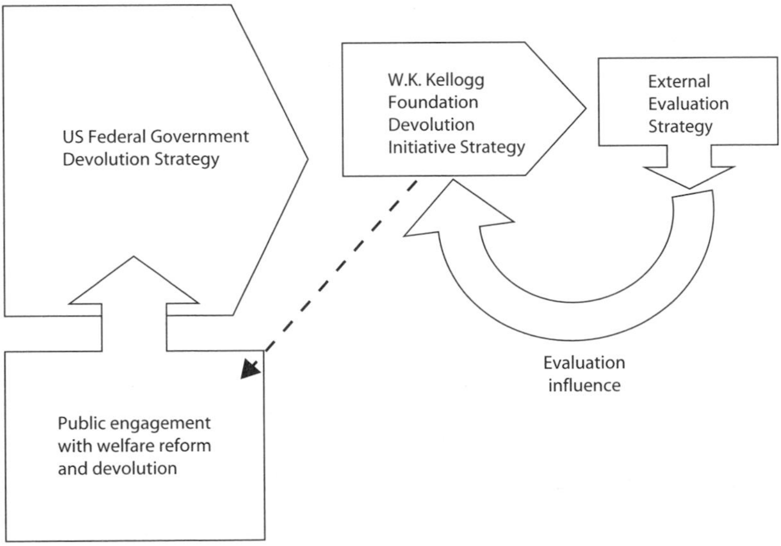

Context and Strategy: Case Study of Devolution

In the fall of 1996, the U.S. federal government embarked on a journey called "devolution"—shifting powers, responsibilities, and funding from the federal level of government to the state level, and sometimes the local level, for a number of social welfare programs, beginning with the cash assistance program for low-income families formerly known as Aid to Families with Dependent Children (AFDC), often called "welfare." The embarkation event, a law called the Personal Responsibility and Work Opportunities Reconciliation Act (PRWORA), was radical—overturning a social safety net that had been built over several decades. And it was politically divisive because the shift of authority away from the federal government was accompanied by a shift from an open-ended system of income assistance for all who were eligible to one with budget limits, time limits for people receiving cash assistance, and requirements for cash assistance recipients to work. Advocates for low-income families worried that PRWORA would leave many destitute and their children consigned to foster care; public policy analysts worried that states, now freer to set welfare policies, would begin "a race to the bottom" to reduce benefits and assistance to low-income families; the authors of the PRWORA legislation worried that Congressional intent would be undermined by liberals in government and in nonprofit entities seeking to "soften" the work requirements and time limits included in the law.

Soon after this historic welfare reform was signed into law by President Bill Clinton, who had promised in his 1992 presidential campaign to "end welfare as we know it," the W. K. Kellogg Foundation began its own devolution journey, eventually committing 7 years and $56 million to a project with 31 grantees, its Devolution Initiative, as well as $3.6 million to an external evaluation of the initiative.

This case looks at the DI and its external evaluation reframed through the lens of strategy. The Initiative was originally described by the Foundation as a project that would track the processes and outcomes of shifting governmental authority and decisions, with the aim of empowering citizens to participate in local and state decisions about issues affecting their lives. As stated in the Foundation's announcement of the Initiative by Foundation President William C. Richardson, "Devolution is about more than the transference of authority. To be truly effective in the long run, devolution is about finding new ways to engage citizens in the process. But, first, they must be informed" (W. K. Kellogg Foundation, 1996a).

In retrospect, the DI can also be seen as an example of using evaluation as a strategic intervention aimed at bringing accountability to the governmental devolution process. In effect, the DI and its external evaluation together constituted an evaluation strategy to help people look over the shoulders of government as a momentous change was under way.

The challenge of the DI in bringing evaluation tools to the goal of accountability was where to look when there were multiple policies and policy-making processes that might be examined. Although PRWORA introduced specific policy and program revisions, the devolution of authority to states and localities injected important elements of process and participation to the welfare-reform agenda. Devolution, the policy change, led to a cascade of considerations about "who is involved and what they are saying and doing"—and how some of those actors should be encouraged and assisted to participate. For the Kellogg Foundation, these considerations became at least as important to the story of welfare reform, for a while, as the state-by-state policy and program outcomes. And they were central to the Kellogg Foundation's evolving design of the DI and its external evaluation.

In revisiting this story in 2010, the policy and program results of the 1996 Congressional welfare reform are under scrutiny. Caseloads for Temporary Assistance for Needy Families (TANF), the program that replaced AFDC under the 1996 reform, and caseloads for AFDC just prior to the reform, declined steadily from mid-1994 to mid-2008 (U.S. Department of Health and Human Services, 2009), and the number of families receiving food stamps (now called the Supplemental Nutritional Assistance Program)—a form of public assistance whose governance structure was not affected by the 1996 law—increased to the point where 1 in 8 Americans and 1 in 4 American children were estimated to receive this assistance in 2009 and about 6 million families receiving food assistance reported that they have zero monthly income—that is, they are living on food stamps alone (DeParle & Gebeloff, 2010). Whether other sources of support are filling the gap and exactly how people with no cash income are getting by has yet to be fully documented.

Looking back on concerns about the potential effects of welfare reform in 2002, Kellogg Foundation President Richardson said,

> Even as perhaps the biggest economic boom in history swept the nation, we wondered how Temporary Assistance to Needy Families would fare when the economy faltered. Even as stocks rose to record highs, we asked what would happen if lower tax revenues required states to cut transportation and child-care supports to the working poor. Even when some financial advisors thought a bear market was unlikely, we questioned how the new safety net programs would function during a lukewarm stage of the business cycle. (Richardson, 2002)

If such worries motivated the Foundation in kicking off the DI in 1997, they proved prescient more than a decade later.

A Case of Evaluation as Strategic Intervention: Devolution Policy Aims, Devolution Initiative Aims

The Law and the Legislative History of Devolution

Devolution, although tied to specific welfare reforms, was at least as much based on political principles as aimed at policy or program objectives. It was characterized by those closest to the Congressional action as another chapter in the history of American government federalism in relation to social policy. In contrast to the long run of increasing federal government responsibility for social welfare programs set off by the Social Security Act of 1935, the 1996 "devolution revolution," authored and led by Republicans, represented a return of authorities and responsibilities to state and local governments for a substantial portion of the country's safety net for the poorest Americans.

The strategy of the Congressional Republicans was centered on who got to make policy decisions, within a framework of changes to the terms of public assistance. In this, Congressional Republicans shaping welfare reform listened closely to governors who wanted more control of their welfare caseloads, their welfare expenditures, and the means to enforce a social obligation to work (Haskins, 2008) (When the welfare reform legislative work got under way in 1994, 30 states were led by Republican governors.) Some assumptions about how devolution would play out at the state and local levels included that those governors had a large fiscal stake in reducing welfare caseloads and promoting work by welfare recipients—which worried opponents to the new rules. But overall, the fact of shifting decision making on this aspect of social policy was seen by the authors of welfare reform as *enabling* fundamental change, but not legislating it in detail. And the fact that President Clinton and his administration eventually agreed to the broad outlines of the Republican Congress's provisions aimed at establishing a culture of work in place of cash entitlements cemented the message of welfare reform: States (and localities) would decide the details of changes, but the prominence of work as a route to self-sufficiency was elevated and the temporary nature of cash assistance was affirmed.

Within the context of the requirements and choices it provided to states, the driving philosophy of devolution was that states (and localities) were better able to craft programs that were appropriate for their constituents and conditions and better able to manage and monitor implementation than federal bureaucrats. At a deeper level, longstanding Republican beliefs in smaller government and the 1994 Republican takeover of the House of Representatives and the Senate gave power to the philosophical commitment to reduce social spending and particularly to reduce the collection of "entitlements" that government had created for Americans of all classes and categories (Haskins, 2008).

The specific changes to the welfare system that states were required to implement included a 5-year lifetime limit on receipt by individuals of federally funded public assistance and a requirement that nonexempt recipients of TANF would participate in work-related activities, including assigned jobs in public and nonprofit agencies, at least 30 hours per week. These requirements were accompanied in the law by a block-grant funding methodology that gave states choices about how to spend federal and state "welfare dollars," which included cash assistance dollars, funds for emergency needs for

TANF applicants and working TANF recipients, and funds for employment assistance (formerly the JOBS program). A separate block grant combined several child-care funding streams and provided states some flexibility to transfer funds between block-grant purposes. States were required to meet standards for the percentage of welfare recipients involved in mandated work-related activities, but they were relatively free to design their own programs of "welfare reform." Devolution left most of the choices up to states (Haskins, 2006; Weaver, 2000).

In addition to cash assistance for low-income families, "devolved" by the 1996 law, the Balanced Budget Act of 1997 authorized federally funded health insurance coverage for children to be designed and managed by states under the State Children's Health Insurance Program (SCHIP). SCHIP became one of the policies tracked by the DI and its external evaluation.

The W. K. Kellogg Foundation's Response to Devolution

The DI of the W. K. Kellogg Foundation, established in response to the 1996 federal law, did not have specific policy or program objectives. Instead, the Kellogg Foundation, referring to its historic mission of helping people help themselves, set out to ensure that the communities and peoples most likely to be affected by decisions on social welfare issues newly in the province of states and localities could find out about proposed changes in laws and regulations and weigh in on those changes effectively. The Kellogg Foundation's Devolution Initiative thus financed the development and dissemination of information as well as capacity building among both research and advocacy organizations at state and local levels to ensure that the voices and perspectives of affected communities and peoples would be heard in the new state and local decision-making arenas.

The Kellogg Foundation had historically focused on communities and community-level issues, and had historically been disinclined to engage public policy issues. The Foundation was also historically reluctant to support research, including policy research. But, as national welfare reform and devolution were being discussed, a convergence of events and changes in the Foundation led to an interest in devolution and related research.

First, Bill Richardson had been hired as the new Foundation president in 1995. As a scholar of health care policy, Board Chair of the Kaiser Family Foundation, and former President of Johns Hopkins University, Richardson had a long-standing interest in public policy. In anticipation of major changes in the nation's social safety net promoted by President Bill Clinton, Richardson created a task force to look at what the Foundation might do to highlight the policy changes for the communities historically of interest to the Foundation. Second, several leading national research institutions were shopping proposals to funders to gather resources to study the effects of devolution, and Richardson wanted to find a way to contribute to these studies that would fit the Foundation's mission and strengths. Third,

Richardson had initiated a restructuring of the Foundation intended to eliminate independent "fiefdoms," increase coordination across programs, and increase the impact of the Foundation's programs. A large, cross-foundation initiative, the DI, provided a structure for these organizational changes to be tested.

Research and Advocacy Projects Funded Under the Devolution Initiative

The Foundation staff began the Initiative with a concept that married the historic Foundation mission to "help people help themselves through the practical application of knowledge and resources to improve their quality of life and that of future generations" with the emerging policy landscape of devolution. They assumed that actors in state, local, and tribal arenas would need information to help them make and influence the making of good policy in the circumstances of devolution. Thus, producing, disseminating, and building capacity to use information effectively was at the heart of the Foundation's DI. The 31 DI grantees played various roles in an information-based strategy to shape policy. "Partners," as the grantees were called, included:

- National nonprofit research institutions conducting national research to study the effects of devolution on low-income families. These groups included the Urban Institute, the Nelson A. Rockefeller Institute of Government at the State University of New York–Albany, MDRC, the Hudson Institute, and Johns Hopkins University's Department of Sociology.
- National policy research organizations tracking and interpreting changes in laws, regulations, funding, programs, demographics, and other trends related to devolution. These groups included the Center on Budget and Policy Priorities, the Center for Law and Social Policy, the Center for Community Change, the Center for Policy Alternatives, the Joint Center for Political and Economic Studies, the National Conference of State Legislatures, and the National Governors' Association.
- National advocacy organizations—some with state affiliates—tracking the potential effects of devolution on particular populations or existing service programs and working to minimize harms and maximize benefits for these populations and service programs as states, localities, and tribes made decisions about welfare, health care, and other social safety net issues. These groups included Families USA, the National Association of Child Advocates (now called Voices for America's Children), the National Coalition on Health Care, the National Congress of American Indians, the Immigrant Welfare Implementation Collaborative, and the Children's Defense Fund.
- State advocacy groups—some affiliated with national advocacy organizations—in Florida, Mississippi, Montana, New York, Washington,

and Wisconsin working to shape state, local, and tribal social safety net policies.

Connected to an emphasis on information, the Foundation staff saw in devolution new opportunities for citizen participation in government; in line with the historic mission, it was assumed that the people who would be affected by devolution of social and health care policies should be encouraged and empowered to participate in the state, local, tribal, and national decisions affecting them, their families, and their communities. Although citizen mobilization and coalition building were envisioned as key activities of the Initiative from the outset, it was not originally envisioned that the Foundation would fund state-level advocacy groups to do this work. Initially, the assumption was that by funding national advocacy organizations and linking them to national research and policy analysis groups, the DI would generate policy-oriented activity in 40 states because the national advocacy grantees had affiliates or related entities in that many states. (Even though the Initiative funded advocacy organizations, the Foundation was notably *not* promoting any particular policy, taking care to avoid prohibited lobbying activity.)

The DI goals, as set forth in a progress report to the Foundation's Board in 1999, were stated as:

Creating an objective information base about the impact of devolution.

Sharing the findings with policymakers and the public.

Using the information and other community resources to promote public participation in informing policy agenda and decisions. (W. K. Kellogg Foundation, 1999)

Evaluation of the Devolution Initiative

The Kellogg Foundation engaged the Harvard Family Research Project (HFRP) to evaluate its DI. This evaluation was necessarily not focused on specific policy results, because the Foundation's activities did not have specific policy objectives. The evaluation was designed to follow and map occasions and paths of policy engagement and influence at the state and local government levels, including the Kellogg Foundation–funded precursors to such engagement and influence—the production and dissemination of policy-relevant information. Not surprisingly, the DI evaluators were challenged by how to judge success when policy outcomes were not specified but engagement and influence—and the more ephemeral "voice" and "empowerment"—were DI objectives. And also not surprisingly, as time passed and expenditures increased, the evaluators were challenged to produce information that demonstrated the value of the Foundation's investment.

This case points to some of the difficulties involved in evaluating a strategy intervention in a public policy arena when expected or desired strategy outcomes were not specified in conventional ways. At the time of the DI evaluation, the set of tools available to evaluators did not include tested models for strategy-focused initiatives lacking specific outcomes. The Kellogg Foundation's devolution journey provides insights into this challenging environment. Although there were complicating factors having to do with the Foundation's structure—such as whether evaluators were expected to have an independent voice—the main focus is on the question of how evaluators can interact with, inform, and ultimately measure the results of policy-oriented initiatives that do not have specific policy outcomes as their goal. And, not the least difficult, is the distinction between strategy and policy—which was often blurry in the DI and its external evaluation. Although the Foundation initially aimed at process, participation, and voice, informed by new information, it ended up concerned about the effects of these strategies on actual policies.

Initiative and Evaluation: Coevolution

The DI and its external evaluation intentionally unfolded together—and in this retrospective review, are together considered a strategic intervention in the devolution policy process. The devolution policy was seen by Foundation staff as extremely complex, but not predictable in 1996, and the Foundation wanted an evaluation to help guide its work on the Initiative—essentially another set of eyes and ears on what was happening with the devolution policy.

The Initiative: A Focus on Informing Policy

The Foundation's early decisions about the Initiative arose from two sources. One source was the deliberations and explorations of a cross-foundation team formed in 1996. Alice Warner described the team's starting point in this way: "We didn't do policy, we didn't do cross-foundation work, and we didn't do research." Nevertheless, a task force that included 15–20 program directors began a series of meetings to "see how to do cross-foundation programming" around devolution, according to Warner, and made decisions resulting in a July 1996 request to the Foundation's Board for the first of what would be four appropriations for the Devolution Initiative. Five grants were proposed to support two nonprofit research institutions and three national advocacy organizations. The task force formed a Core Team for decision making in late 1996. (Warner started out as a contracted advisor to the DI team and became the assistant to team's codirectors.)

A second source was a brief premises paper that laid the foundations for the DI and its evaluation: The premises, described below, were all about participation, process, and learning—not about policy and program outcomes.

Premise 1: While devolution creates new potential for citizen involvement, participation in devolution processes can be enhanced by increasing the capacity and confidence of grassroots and local leaders to influence policy. Capacity building is an activity that can be effectively carried out by intermediary organizations with statewide coalitions. (W. K. Kellogg Foundation, 1996b)

Premise 2: It is possible to build essential learning relationships among a set of grantees. Through the Devolution Strategy, the grantees will produce, enhance, and capture information from their constituencies and target audiences and get information to them in a two-way facilitated exchange of information. Innovative means and creative channels of dissemination will need to be pursued which facilitate moving relevant information to the right people at the right time. The grantees will build individual and collective knowledge that will provide ongoing influence in decision-making processes regarding devolution, and will reach and involve other groups in their learning process. However, we recognize that information packaging, dissemination, and utilization are necessary—but by themselves insufficient—to galvanize participation in policy processes.

Premise 3: The Devolution Strategy represents an innovative form of grant making for WKKF because it combines in a single strategy, information producers, advocacy organizations, a policy focus, and the involvement of program directors from multiple programming areas across the Foundation. We want to learn the extent to which grant making can create interrelationships among nontraditional partner grantees as a result of our investment that go beyond the activities of individual projects. In other words, we intend to determine if it is possible to create working conditions among the grantees that will yield policy effects such that the sum is greater than individual contributions.

Premise 4: Devolution is likely to cause significant changes in relationships between nonprofit organizations, government at all levels, and philanthropy. The devolution strategy is an opportunity for the WKKF to participate in a coevolutionary process with its five grantee partners that will ultimately allow each participant to continue to be an effective player in a devolved world. WKKF's funding presence in devolution creates unique opportunities for organizational learning that will allow WKKF to be responsive to a changing environment while at the same time remaining true to its mission of helping people help themselves.

This premises document was the first step—described as a "learning manifesto" by Alice Warner, one of its authors—in developing a logic model for the Initiative, which would evolve as the initiative and evaluation evolved. At the time the document was developed, the intermediary organizations

Figure 4.2. A Model for the Devolution Initiative

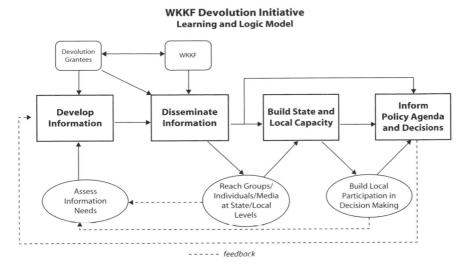

------ *feedback*

referred to in Premise 1 were *national* organizations, assumed to have the capacity to speak to state and local audiences—a premise that would later be revisited. Also, the concept and structure of the Devolution Initiative described in this document was being retrofitted to an existing set of grantees because five grants for devolution research and advocacy had been made in July 1996, before the "Premises Paper" was prepared.

In this early stage of creating the DI, the decision was also made to manage it internally rather than to engage an intermediary organization—in part, to use the DI experience to practice cross-foundation work. To aid the internal thinking and management, consultants were brought in to advise on several aspects of the Initiative, including consultant firms specializing in policy and communications that stayed with the DI over its course. In addition, Heather Weiss of the Harvard Family Research Project was brought in to advise on an evaluation and learning strategy. Weiss's organization was eventually selected in late 1997 to conduct an outside evaluation of the Initiative.

The first of several versions of the DI logic model was included in an evaluation proposal by the Harvard Family Research Project (HFRP) to the Foundation in October 1997. Based on the statements of the premises paper and conversations with Foundation staff, the model set out the strategy and expected outcomes of the DI as depicted in Figure 4.2.

The Evaluation: A Focus on Learning About Grantees' Informing Policy

In its October 1997 proposal, the HFRP evaluators put forth the following questions for addressing the impact of the DI:

(1) Is information reaching the intended audiences? Are different audiences finding it useful? What else do they need?

(2) Are information providers adapting the type, form, or timing of information in light of evolving customer needs? Is a critical mass of information available to meet customer needs and stimulate diverse stakeholder interest and engagement?

(3) Is the information getting to intermediary organizations? Are intermediary organizations building the capacity of groups to use information?

(4) Are a range of groups getting and using information to inform policy discussion, development, and modification?

(5) Is there evidence the Initiative is working so that policymakers are using information and stakeholder input to inform the policy agenda and decisions? (HFRP, 1997, p. 4)

HFRP's evaluation used mixed (quantitative and qualitative) and multiple methods to assess the DI's complex layers. The evaluators also used triangulation—the use of multiple methods and/or data sources to study the same phenomenon—to examine the DI's intended outcomes and corroborate findings.

The process of arriving at this evaluation plan and the process of carrying it out involved complicated issues of attribution—what could be learned and what was actually learned about the "value added" of the Foundation's investments in the Devolution Initiative.

The HFRP evaluators believed that a fresh evaluation approach underscoring collaboration, continuous feedback, learning, and flexibility was more appropriate than traditional evaluation approaches. As the HFRP proposal stated:

> The nature of the Initiative—particularly its evolving character, diffuse "treatment" and probable "contamination" of the treatment by other non-WKKF information and capacity-building efforts—is such that experimental or comparison group designs are not feasible. Therefore, it will not be possible to make definitive causal statements about the impact of the Initiative.
>
> The proposed design provides data to test whether a *plausible* and *credible* case can be made that the Initiative worked as modeled and positively affected the nature, availability and use of information as intended. (HFRP, 1997, p. 7)

The evaluators further noted that attribution of changes in policy to the DI investments would not have been possible because several other national foundations were funding the DI grantee organizations to do the same or similar work across the country. An evaluation design was chosen with both formative and summative components. In its formative approach, the evaluation was intended to provide timely, continuous feedback to the Foundation based on both qualitative and quantitative data collection about the initiative as a whole, including how grantee activities were—or were not—adding up to the DI strategy envisioned by the Foundation. In addition, the evaluation was intended to facilitate clarification of grantees' goals; create a learning system among grantees, consultant partners, and the involved Foundation staff; and provide suggestions and assistance for "continuous improvement." The evaluation was planned as a mechanism for strategic thinking about the DI throughout its course, to help the Foundation manage the initiative by feeding information to a Core Team making decisions about next steps.

The HFRP team leaders characterized the situation going into the evaluation in this way:

> From the outset, the Initiative raised formidable challenges for both the Foundation and its evaluation. First, the cross-foundation team approach to grant making was completely uncharted territory. A process for collective and collaborative decision making did not exist. Second, existing grants were retrofitted into a new initiative in which grantees were expected to work together, in addition to completing the terms of their original grants. The Foundation was challenged to make the whole of the Devolution Initiative greater than the sum of its individual parts. Evaluators were expected to help create as well as track "the whole." Third, the funding of policy work and advocacy was a new direction for the Foundation. Fourth, there were many questions about how best to evaluate a complex initiative and particularly one that involved advocacy and policy. New approaches, such as theory of change evaluation, were emerging but had not been widely tested. Fifth, the approach of involving evaluators from the start was a relatively new one within the Foundation, particularly with respect to the evaluation's relationship to the cross-foundation leadership team. And, finally, all of this was taking place within an environment of restructuring and downsizing within the Foundation, which meant that membership on the Foundation's core leadership team shifted over the course of the Initiative. (Author interview with H. Weiss and J. Coffman, October 4, 2004)

The downsizing at the Foundation began in 1997, as a process of reducing its staff and grant portfolios, with the goal of reducing both by about half due to declines in Kellogg company stock, which constituted about 70% of the Foundation's assets at that point.

One method of strategy support by the evaluators for the Initiative focused on reviewing and refining the DI logic model. According to the evaluators, this helped structure conversations in the DI core team about different ways in which the DI could develop. The logic model was revised several times, and elaborated, over the course of the Initiative. The underlying evolution of the Foundation team's thinking confirmed for the evaluators the emerging nature of the Initiative as the devolution policy landscape clarified, and thus confirmed as well the need for a formative evaluation design. According to Heather Weiss, "We recognized at the outset that much about the Initiative would change over time, and that the evaluation would need to help inform those changes as well as adjust to them. We didn't anticipate, however, the extent of the changes that would come."

The Evaluation End Game: It Really Is About the Impacts

Early in the development of the external evaluation, Ricardo Millett, the Foundation's evaluation director, noted that "attribution" was not a primary objective of the evaluation. He also pointed to the evaluators' challenge to satisfy multiple Foundation clients: Even though Millett did not think an experimental evaluation approach made any sense for an initiative finding its way in an emerging policy landscape, the Foundation's co-chairs of the DI were frequently asked by Board members what difference DI was making and how the Foundation staff would know.

The summative component of the evaluation became more prominent late in the DI course in order to respond to this concern, but, in the view of several Foundation observers, it did not fully succeed in answering the question about the initiative's impact. Although some observers concluded that the evaluation emphasized learning about information flow and the utility of information for advocacy, rather than the results of information on policy, the external evaluators disagree. And Millett concurs with the evaluators that they "tried hard to make the connection between the DI activities and policy outcomes." The HFRP evaluators cite their tracking of 22 policies in 1999–2000 and 47 policies in 2000–2001, combined with quantitative and qualitative state-level data collection, as their efforts to determine if a plausible case could be made that the DI grantee efforts contributed to policy outcomes. The evaluators reported that the "intended policy results" were achieved for 17 of the 22 issues that grantees informed in 1999–2000 and 32 of 47 issues in 2000–2001 (HFRP, 2002, p. 31).

In the final stage of the DI, the Foundation employed a communications strategy to answer the question of impact. Materials accompanying the final appropriation request to the Board for the DI told "stories" of new voices in state and local policy decisions and the human face of the Initiative— stories that were prepared by the Foundation's Communications unit, not the evaluators. The public story of the DI was also told in a Communications unit produced book, not a final evaluation report (W. K. Kellogg Foundation, 2001).

The Evaluation: An Indistinct Bottom Line

Much of the evolution of the Initiative and its external evaluation can be understood in the context of the Foundation staff's response to the shortcomings they came to recognize in the initial strategy—shortcomings the evaluators uncovered and brought to the attention of the DI core team, in their view. It turned out that the funded national research institutions were accustomed to speaking to a national policy audience and were, in some cases, unsuited for the task of producing policy information useful for advocacy organizations, in general, and specifically for the state and local players in devolution. It also turned out that national advocacy organizations, in some cases, did not have the resources, or the requisite relationships with each other or with their own local affiliates, to lead capacity building for effective state and local coalition building and citizen mobilization. In response, 2 years into the Initiative, the Foundation added a new set of grants and activities to build capacity for informing policy at the state and local levels of decision making. Further into the Initiative, a Scholar/Practitioner program was added to support state and local policy research and serve as a policy training ground for minority scholars.

The result of these and other decisions was that the Initiative got complicated and, consequently, the external evaluation of the Initiative got complicated. As several people interviewed for this case said, referring to either the Initiative or its external evaluation—or the two together: "It had a lot of moving parts." In the end, the complicated DI strategy and an evaluation designed to keep track of all the moving parts—but not to sum up its impact—contributed to an indistinct "bottom line."

The Evaluation Intervention Strategy

The W. K. Kellogg Foundation leaders interested in the issue of devolution of social-policy decision making in 1996 and 1997 did not set out to employ evaluation as a strategic intervention to hold government accountable for social policy decisions; nor did the Foundation actors articulate that its external evaluation of the DI would be the means for assessing the effectiveness of such a strategic intervention. The language was different then—focused on information gathering and dissemination—and the boundaries of evaluation territory were different then. Nevertheless, today, the DI and its companion external evaluation can together be seen as just such an evaluation-based strategic intervention. One bit of evidence supporting this interpretation is the final illustration of the Initiative's theory of change, produced by the evaluators. This illustration starts with "dissemintion of information"—for the most part, research-based information gathered by evaluators who were Foundation grantees (see Figure 4.3).

Pathway 1 was the most direct route to informing policy, with a line from grantees (in this case, national grantees) and their information to informing policy. Pathway 2 also informed policy, but reflected an investment in building unified voices among state and community advocates to do it. Later DI investments in state grantees and their community-based partners gave legs to and pushed for results along Pathway 2. Pathway 3

Figure 4.3. Pathways to Informing Policy

Pathway 1: National grantees inform policy through information development and dissemination.

Pathway 2: State grantees and their community-based partners inform policy.

Pathway 3: State grantees and their community-based partners build the capacity of citizens and new voices to inform policy.

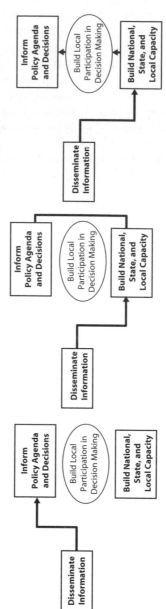

drilled down deeper into communities and reflected an investment in state grantees and their community-based partners to build capacity of community members, particularly new voices underrepresented in the policy process, to inform policy.

In this final theory of change for the DI, information is seen as the instigator of action leading to participation in policy development and ultimate policy decision making. Today, methods of organizing for policy change and methods of disseminating information to support the participation of affected peoples and communities are quite different from what they were in 1996, when the Devolution Initiative began. But the DI experience still suggests that an evaluation aimed at interpreting and funneling information to a strategy-formulating body, such as the DI core team, can constitute a strategic intervention. In the Kellogg Foundation's DI, the role of the evaluation had not been worked out in these terms and there were difficult struggles to define what the evaluators were expected to contribute. Looking through the lens of evaluation as a strategic intervention, the DI and its external evaluation offer a new lesson about how to keep an eye on the prize—in this case, participation in policy making and policy outcomes.

References

DeParle, J., & Gebeloff, R. M. (2010, January 3). Living on nothing but food stamps. *New York Times*, p. A1.

Harvard Family Research Project. (1997, October 10). *W. K. Kellogg Foundation Devolution Initiative evaluation proposal.*

Harvard Family Research Project. (2002, February). *W. K. Kellogg Foundation's Devolution Initiative: Learning report, 1997–2001 evaluation findings.*

Haskins, R. (2006). *Work over welfare: The inside story of the 1996 welfare reform law.* Washington, DC: Brookings Institution Press.

Haskins, R. (2008). Governors and the development of American social policy. In E. G. Sribnick (Ed.), *A legacy of innovation: Governors and public policy* (pp. 76–103). Philadelphia: University of Pennsylvania.

Patrizi, P., & Patton, M. Q. (Eds.). (2005). *Teaching evaluation using the case method. New Directions for Evaluation, 105.*

Richardson, W. C. (2002, January). *Devolution: The end of the beginning.* Speech presented at the Devolution Initiative Conference, Washington, DC.

Sherwood, K. E. (2005a). Evaluating home visitation: A case study of evaluation at the The David and Lucile Packard Foundation. *Teaching evaluation using the case method. New Directions for Evaluation, 105,* 59–81.

Sherwood, K. E. (2005b). Evaluation of the Fighting Back Initiative. *New Directions for Evaluation, 105,* 15–38.

U.S. Department of Health and Human Services, Administration for Children and Families, Office of Family Assistance, Temporary Assistance for Needy Families. (2009). *Caseload data 2000–2008.* Retrieved from http://www.acf.hhs.gov/programs/ofa/data-reports/caseload/caseload_recent.html

Weaver, R. K. (2000). *Ending welfare as we know it.* Washington, DC: Brookings Institution Press.

W. K. Kellogg Foundation. (1996a, July 31). *Kellogg Foundation announces program to inform devolution policies* (news release). Battle Creek, MI: Author.

W. K. Kellogg Foundation. (1996b, December 18). *Devolution Initiative premise paper.* Battle Creek, MI: Author.

W. K. Kellogg Foundation. (1999, April 14–15). *The Devolution Initiative: Application of knowledge to the problems of people, a program initiative progress report.* Battle Creek, MI: Author.

W. K. Kellogg Foundation. (2001). *Building bridges between people and policy: Devolution in practice, lessons from the W. K. Kellogg Foundation's Devolution Initiative.* Battle Creek, MI: Author.

KAY E. SHERWOOD is an independent consultant to public and nonprofit organizations based in New Jersey.

NEW DIRECTIONS FOR EVALUATION • DOI: 10.1002/ev

Patrizi, P. A. (2010). Strategy evaluation: Emerging processes and methods. In P. A. Patrizi &
M. Q. Patton (Eds.), *Evaluating strategy. New Directions for Evaluation, 128*, 87–102.

5

Strategy Evaluation: Emerging Processes and Methods

Patricia A. Patrizi

Abstract

*This chapter offers reflections on and lessons about methods for conducting
strategy evaluation based on and extracted from various strategy evaluations.
The approach offered builds on both reflective practice and developmental evaluation. The chapter operationalizes the Minztberg framework for the social sector and addresses issues such as how to consider strategy boundaries, the
strategy-making entity, sources and types of data, unit of analysis, and types of
analysis. It offers ideas about how to apply the approach in evaluations of both
a retrospective or prospective nature.* © Wiley Periodicals, Inc., and the American Evaluation Association.

T he focus on strategy in philanthropy and government is widespread
and growing. A recent survey conducted by the Evaluation Roundtable surfaces what appears to be increased demand by foundation
executives for information and assessment regarding all things deemed
strategic (Patrizi, 2010). And although a great deal has been written about
strategy, there is virtually nothing in the literature to guide us on how to
evaluate strategy, particularly as it relates to strategy of social benefit.
Mintzberg (2007) is the best source for guidance as to how to evaluate strategy. As in the past, with this increasing reliance on strategy as the focus of
program operators and funders, evaluators have been compelled to be
inventive in their approach to this new evaluand. The profession has faced

analogous challenges. For example, cluster evaluation was created to respond to the need for evaluating across different projects, and metaevaluation evolved to evaluate evaluations.

The purpose of this chapter is to describe an approach to evaluating strategy and the challenges associated with the work. This chapter builds on Chapter 3, which discusses an evaluation of the Robert Wood Johnson investment to improve care at the end of life. In the first part of this chapter, I reflect on the challenges encountered in the end-of-life strategy evaluation, which reminds us in some ways of the fable of the blind men and the elephant. In this tale, a group of blind men touch an elephant to learn what it is like. Each one touches a different part, but only one part, such as the ear, tail, side, or tusk. The men then compare notes and learn that they are in complete disagreement about the nature of the elephant.

Such is the case with strategy. Depending on a multitude of factors, the definition of strategy can be subject to broad interpretation. "Strategy" for one actor is not strategy for another, even within the same organization. Across organizations, the divergence of views on what constitutes strategy is dramatic. Our difficulty in defining the strategy guiding the Robert Wood Johnson Foundation's (RWJF) work to improve end-of-life care is revealing of the complex challenges encountered in assessments of these kind. In the second part of this chapter, we share an emerging approach to strategy evaluation that evolved from the RWJF evaluation and the Evaluation Roundtable's work with Henry Mintzberg.

What Is Strategy? Defining the Robert Wood Johnson's End-of-Life Strategy

In conducting the RWJF strategy assessment (presented as a case study in Chapter 3), we began with a straightforward set of questions:

> What was the strategy? How did the strategy evolve?
> What did the strategy achieve?
> Who were the key actors in the strategy?

For the purposes of the assignment, we used a rough working definition of strategy: that is, *all efforts that more or less align toward a goal*. We started where many evaluators begin—by attempting to understand the nature of the work as fully as possible. Toward this end, we

> Interviewed current RWJF staff to solicit their descriptions of the strategy—what they did and toward what end.
> Searched for what we called "framing documents" that might describe what the Foundation did and why.
> Reviewed material describing grants made and results of the grants; we looked for indications that elements of the work had intersected.

NEW DIRECTIONS FOR EVALUATION • DOI: 10.1002/ev

Sought to understand the objectives of the work and their role in defining and advancing "the strategy."

From this, we hoped to develop a landscape of the grant making that fell into clusters or what we came to call "lines of work." We expected to see linkages among the lines of work. However, this first-level review did not yield what we expected. Instead, we identified six key themes that may apply more generally when evaluating strategy.

Theme 1: No Organizational or Collective View on Strategy

Our interviews with current Foundation staff provided us with fairly bounded views of the strategy, telling us, in effect, what each person did. We then expanded our focus to include former RWJF staff and several of those outside the Foundation who were considered "key" to the development and execution of the strategy. From this set of conversations, we realized that our initial set of grants to review—some 30 grants—reflected, inadequately and incompletely, just one historical body of work. But the linkages between it and earlier related RWJF supported efforts were missing. We also came to the conclusion that current and past staff members often interpreted strategy as a limited reflection of their own experience. There is no new "insight" in the revelation that anything open to interpretation can and will be understood subjectively, rather than as objective reality. Yet when it comes to strategy, many believe that a collective consciousness will prevail.

**Theme 2: Strategy May Not Be Limited to the Actors
or the Space and Time Considered**

Initially, the Foundation identified 30 grants as the focus for our evaluation, but this selection left out important learning that had taken place before the grants. From the Foundation's point of view these 30 grants were pivotal in terms of output, but we came to see that their success was built on the experience of hundreds of preceding grants as well as the Foundation's cumulative learning in making them. We came to understand that significant elements were left out of the initial scoping of the strategy in part to make the evaluation doable, but also because the earlier work fell out of the line of vision of the first strategists we interviewed.

We learned that the historical grant making had value, not only as a frame of reference, but because it played an active role in the Foundation's strategic perspective at the time. The earlier grant making shaped how the rest of the field understood the issues, as well as the Foundation's role in addressing them.

The phase of the Foundation's end-of-life work that we had been asked to assess followed what RWJF considered to be the failure of SUPPORT, a $31 million study begun in 1988 to understand the problems of patients

NEW DIRECTIONS FOR EVALUATION • DOI: 10.1002/ev

who died in hospitals and a subsequent randomized controlled trial to address the deficiencies in care. The fact that SUPPORT's interventions did not yield the expected outcomes deeply influenced four aspects of Foundation strategy development going forward. The major changes were:

Moving from a highly prescribed way of working—investing in one major programmatic response, that is, the funding of a randomized controlled (RCT) trial—to a far less certain approach (called "a collective head scratch" by one foundation leader).

Programming directions took over 2 years to emerge and involved a "close to the ground" manner of working, as opposed to the in-house design work that characterized the development of SUPPORT.

Expanding the focus from one major effort (SUPPORT) to investing in a far more varied set of approaches to the issue.

Shifting from investing millions in an RCT to investing very modestly on evaluation. In an interview, one staff member reflected on this phenomenon as "research fatigue" that set in after SUPPORT.

Despite the apparent failure of SUPPORT's interventions, the primary and secondary research that emanated from the project had a major impact. The data comprise what many have called the most authoritative body of knowledge about death in America that exists to this day. Many in the field attribute the call for change in care of the dying to the Robert Wood Johnson Foundation's involvement in SUPPORT, and this is still part of the Foundation's reputation.

Understanding the nature of historical investments provided us with a deeper appreciation of the decisions that were to follow. They were an early indication of the Foundation's strategic perspective and shifts therein, which were in play at the time of the grant making.

Theme 3: Strategy Documents—What You Write May Not Be What You Do

The Foundation began its work in end-of-life care before the current trend of developing theories of change or logic models took hold. However, two major source documents were important. Three years after the strategy was launched, Foundation staff published an article in which they articulated their views about the problems in end-of-life care, what they valued, and their vision for the future (Weisfeld, Miller, Gibson, & Schroeder, 2000). The paper presented the Foundation's three-part strategy focused on: professional education, institutional change, and public engagement. What then followed was the rationale for a range of grants. The article did not describe how change in the three domains would come about.

The Institute of Medicine (IOM), supported in part by RWJF, produced another important framing document, which outlined a vision for future of care of the dying (Field & Cassel, 1997). The IOM is a highly prestigious body in the field of health care and many of its reports come to be thought of as seminal. This was one such report. When queried for a rationale for work in the end-of-life care field, RWJF staff often pointed to the IOM document as a justification for many decisions. The IOM report presented a litany of services and changes needed to improve care, but it offered no guidance on how change would come about.

Although both these documents provided insight into how the Foundation viewed the problems in end-of-life care, they offered little to inform the reader about how the vision would be achieved.

Theme 4: The Failure of Objectives to Reveal Strategy

Ultimately, we reviewed each of the 337 grants that RWJF made in end-of-life care between 1996 and 2005, and we sought to place them within the Foundation's stated funding priorities—as broad as they were. We were somewhat hamstrung by the fact that, at the time the grants were made, the Foundation did not track or code its grants and other investments according to their stated objective areas. We undertook this task and found that many of the grants seemed to fall outside of the three objectives, crossed objectives, or were only loosely connected to them. We were quickly baffled by the complexity, history, and interrelationships of the efforts and found ourselves tangled in a web of ideas and a morass of data.

Theme 5: Strategy Evaluation Is Not Program Evaluation

Strategy usually embodies multiple efforts to reach an end state of some kind. Therefore, evaluation of strategy frequently needs to elevate the focal unit to a level larger than a single program or project. A major challenge for us was to avoid slipping into conducting individual program evaluations. As evaluators, we struggled to elevate our inquiry to the level of strategy and to resist getting mired in project or program effectiveness. In more than one instance, we saw that a program could be highly flawed and not produce intended results, yet it could be successful in yielding outcomes that advanced the broader, field-level strategy. Although we learned as much as we could about program effectiveness, we had to stop to consider our core questions: How did the program contribute to the overall strategy? What role did the program play in the strategy? How did it advance or hinder the overall effort, regardless of its performance in its own right?

Theme 6: Who Is the Strategy-Making Entity?

This evaluation also challenged us to consider the following question: Who was the strategist in the RWJF effort? We quickly discovered that there was no single strategist at the Foundation, and that the strategy was less

NEW DIRECTIONS FOR EVALUATION • DOI: 10.1002/ev

centrally "controlled" by the Foundation than we originally thought. The strategy had numerous architects with varying degrees of influence over decisions and execution. Theories of complexity aside, social investors have some degree of control over their investments, but they have far less control over the work of their grantees. We realized that we needed to understand and factor in both the acknowledged and unacknowledged roles of the many contributing to an effort of this scale.

Identifying Patterns in Actions: The Development of Strategy Hypotheses

After extensive interviewing and document review, we concluded that no one could or would provide us with "the strategy." We turned our attention instead toward understanding strategy through the lens of understanding actions.

Although there was limited information on overall strategic direction, RWJF did not suffer from a lack of material regarding individual grants and initiatives. Particularly valuable were RWJF's Grant Results Reports, which summarize the work carried out under each grant. Written by a team of Foundation consultants, the reports capture much of the rationale behind funded projects, how they were developed, what was accomplished, and what was learned from both the grantee and Foundation perspective.

Although we had abundant good material from the reports, they focused on individual projects and did little to shed light on linkages or interrelationships among the efforts. Although other multiprogram evaluation designs, such as cluster evaluations, look across similar grants, a strategy evaluation needs to examine how an assortment of varied grants and actions align toward a common goal.

To make this kind of judgment about grant alignment, we realized we would need to jog staff memory proactively. This forced us to undertake an extensive analytic task that would help us query staff intelligently about how to interpret the strategic meaning of their grants.

Digging Deeper

To allow for better interpretation of the grants made under the aegis of end of life, we began to code each grant along several dimensions, which we believed would capture a relevant set of who, what, when, where, and how characteristics of the portfolio:

- *Type of organization receiving the funds* (for example, university, trade organization, professional organization, health care provider). This dimension offered us a view to the relative weighting of organizational types. Then, we could address whether Foundation grant making was heavily weighted toward academic settings or was more dispersed throughout the field, whether it leaned toward more formal or informal organizations, and so forth.

- *Site of service delivery* (for example, hospitals, nursing homes, home health, community health centers). This dimension allowed us to examine whether and how the Foundation supported a system of palliative care and to understand the role of the parts. We analyzed the amount of money invested in each service setting, the documents produced, and the types of projects funded. We then looked at the parts to determine whether the Foundation was more or less inclined toward niche grant making or whether staff sought a particular leverage point in the way they approached grant making.
- *Products and processes.* This dimension allowed us to understand the types of work supported, processes that were favored, and whether elements of the work accrued toward much. We could then begin to identify strategy elements and whether the outputs of grants aligned. From this, we were able to discern emerging bodies of predominantly practice-oriented literature essential to building curriculum in end-of-life care. We could link products to people and people to institutions and sources of support. From this we could identify linkages to the Foundation's most important strategic partner.
- *Strategic actors.* We also tracked individuals and institutions as strategic elements in their own right. What did they bring to the effort in terms of influence? What type of authority or status did they command? Who were they known to be able to influence? Who worked with whom?
- *Users and end targets.* We expected this dimension to inform us about the beneficiaries of the change strategy, which would provide an outcomes view to the work. We coded grants along the lines of the three major program objectives as they evolved over time: changes in practice; institutional change; and changes in policy, systems, and professional and consumer will concerning end-of-life care. Also, we looked for patterns in the types of beneficiaries served and desired outcomes as they were discussed in grant documents. Again, we saw a few patterns, but only enough to keep us confused. The analysis yielded more questions than answers, but the questions led us to return to Foundation staff for more inquiry.

Re-creating the Historical Milieu

Time is always an important dimension in strategy evaluation, because strategy plays out over a period of months or years. The most important breakthrough in our analysis came about after we plotted RWJF's 337 individual end-of-life care grants along a timeline that also showed the contemporaneous lead actors and important events such as meetings and release of significant reports or research. The timeline was most revealing because with it we could go back to Foundation staff with questions about particular periods when simultaneous events occurred. This more context-bound approach to interviewing with specific references to events (grants, meetings, papers, etc.) tended to jog memory far better than our previous grant-by-grant or objective-by-objective approach.

NEW DIRECTIONS FOR EVALUATION • DOI: 10.1002/ev

Bringing a broader set of actions and historical realities to our questioning allowed us to probe into the challenges and motivations behind the decisions that were made. This approach elicited detailed stories of the work, often with fine-grain commentary related to staff thinking and learning about their choices. And to our delight, the more detailed historical context triggered information about connections among the grants that had not previously emerged.

Ultimately, a set of core strategies emerged (aligned with time, resource allocation, and strategic actors) that others could recognize and confirm as such. This analysis surfaced important elements of strategy that had previously eluded us, including: elements of position, dynamics of the targeted field (including incentives for behavioral change and systems dynamics), vehicles of leverage, and a beginning appreciation of how perspective is instrumental to strategy and its execution. As a result, we could generate far more sensitive questions and hypotheses than we could previously, and others could validate them as well.

An Emerging Framework for Strategy Evaluation

In this section, we link suggested elements of the review process to concepts from the Mintzberg framework discussed in Chapter 1. We have applied and adapted the framework presented by Mintzberg at the Evaluation Roundtable meeting in 2008. Mintzberg's framework focused on private sector distinctions and examples, and we adapted it to the social sector. Mintzberg focuses on four types of strategy, which he has identified during decades of research: strategy as plan, perspective, position, and pattern. No one category is meant to be mutually exclusive and all have a place in the formulation and execution of strategy. We discuss below how each view on strategy reveals important information about the strategic enterprise.

Strategy as Plan

Plans represent the rational intentions of the strategic actor, usually formulated at one point in time. They offer projections based on assumptions of "knowability" in the world such that aims can be set and met. Mintzberg, a skeptic about plans, is widely credited as having written the final word on corporate planning in his book *The Rise and Fall of Strategic Planning* (Mintzberg, 1994). However, Mintzberg values plans when they are used to guide tactical execution of strategy *following* extensive experience, which he calls "venturing" and learning.

Strategic plans within the social sector often take the form of theories of change and logic models. Evaluators commonly are asked to assess the quality of the theory of change and the achievement of strategy objectives. Far too often, they find themselves assessing achievement of objectives that may not have been correct in the first place. Because what gets measured is usually what gets done, evaluators can find themselves inadvertently obstructing what may be important and possibly essential program adaptation by applying the achievement of objectives as the indicator of success.

For strategy assessment purposes, however, plans provide a useful window into how strategic actors view the world in terms of cause and effect, as well as what they value and believe, and how they treat information to formulate a case. In other words, plans should be treated as *data* rather than a guideline by which to assess performance. They can be used to inform the strategy assessment by shedding light on dynamics around the creation of the plan:

Who or what is in the line of vision of the plan and what level of control is assumed?

Who are the major strategic actors purported to be?

Who drives the plan and sets its terms of reference? Does a single visionary leader or a group of actors drive the plan? Is the plan imposed on others or has a consensus been built?

What kind of evidence is used in the plan to support arguments?

Strategy as Perspective

Perspective reflects a number of internal drivers to strategy, such as values, competencies, beliefs, and preferences related to *how* something should be done and *how* effects are most likely created. For instance, the end-of-life strategy was shaped by a perspective that "elites" drive medicine, and that the medical education system is highly responsive to peer certification pressures. A persistent use of one theory of change—for example, the repeated use of coalitions to solve social problems—can indicate perspective.

Perspective reflects an organization's sense, belief, and judgment about how it can be effective. Perspectives emerge from the body of experience that an institution accrues in conducting its work. In Mintzberg's terms, perspective should only surface after an organization has invested time in venturing and then learning. In strong leadership situations, the perspective of the leader tends to be the perspective of the organization (Mintzberg, 2007). We posit that most organizations have perspectives—some weak, some strong—but, more often than not, they remain largely undeclared and therefore unexamined and untested. When understood well enough, perspective becomes a way of doing business.

To understand strategy, an evaluator needs to probe for perspective, as it is likely not to be acknowledged explicitly. We have found information about perspective in several sources: patterns of action that involve a repeated theory of change or patterns in preferred ways of working, such as top-down or bottom-up or consensus-driven decision making. Leaders' speeches tend to provide examples of perspective, particularly when ideas about change or striking metaphors are used time and again. Other clues to perspective include:

Actors' statements of driving beliefs
Use and meaning of buzz words
Use and meaning of different problem frames

Organizations with strong and well-understood perspectives often use them successfully to make decisions about strategic position, or where they can work most effectively and how.

Several of the strategic questions that can be applied to perspective are:

What is the range of perspectives? Which are dominant? Are any acknowledged or shared? Are perspectives well or commonly understood across the organization?

If there are multiple perspectives, do tensions among them surface and what are they?

How does perspective surface and affect the work (strategy) as it is cast and executed?

Strategy as Position

Position can best be thought of as the location of outcomes. For instance, the field of palliative care was one position; another was hospital care for the dying. Position literally is the place where an organization aims to have an effect, and where it discerns advantages and opportunities to reach outcomes. Without position, it is difficult to consider an outcomes framework because position grounds strategy in terms of performance in space and time.

Strategies may have no position or have so many positions that achievement within any one spot is questionable. Issues with position arise when organizations aim to realize outcomes, but do so without clear enough intentionality such that resources are inordinately diffused. Or the reverse can occur, such as when a strategy is executed with such relentless focus on narrow achievement of its aims that larger system issues are ignored. An example is the worldwide effort to eradicate polio, discussed in the first chapter, in which analysis showed that unless the overall health system was improved in developing countries in support of fighting specific diseases, the narrowly targeted campaign would not succeed (Guth, 2010).

Questions regarding the strategic nature of position include:

What is the locale of investment/resources and how much will be invested?

Is the strategy appropriate for the position chosen? Does the strategy fit the environment chosen?

How complete is implementation of the parts of the strategy in position?

Did shifts in approach occur? How and why?

How did position alter perspective?

Strategy as Pattern

The identification of patterns is the central analytic tool in strategy assessment to generate hypotheses about actions, perspectives, and position. Patterns emerging from what is actually done (in the distant or proximate past) inform us about the forces, thinking, and learning that guide action. Tracking and evaluating strategy requires a commitment to data collection and use, including an investment in coding, plotting, graphing, or analyzing information in multiple ways. Important data about a start or lag in action, or about important environmental events, should be tracked in relation to decisions and time.

Depending on when the evaluation is conducted (retrospectively or prospectively), tracking behavior can lead to important baseline observations—about actions, values, practices, processes, structures, competencies, networks, and beliefs—that can guide a strategy constructively. From the outset, data for patterning should be as tangible as possible.

At the start of the evaluation—focus on basics:

Actions taken and in what time periods—How do they group? Can they be named?
The actors involved—What are their roles? How have roles evolved?
Resources—What has been invested? In what and when?
Organizational types chosen.
People and places.

Beyond the basics—evidence of thinking, interplay, and networks:

Evidence of assumptions related to strategy execution—Other actors, policies, research needed for strategy evolution.
Major decisions made—In what time period and by whom?
Overlap or intersection of efforts.

Linking perspective and position to actions:

Ways of working—Repeated use of certain "means" or theories of change, specific operating styles.
How people and places are connected to the "means" behind the strategy.

Strategy Evaluation and Pattern Recognition

The recognition of patterns is just the first step—coming to understanding and assessment requires more. A pattern can be meaningless until it is juxtaposed against other patterns, responses, or outcomes. For example, we puzzled over the amount of resources invested in hospitals as opposed to home health or hospice care. During conversations with the strategists, we came to appreciate this investment in light of data showing that:

Most people die in hospitals.

The greatest expenditures in health care occur in hospitals for people at the end of life.

Hospitals have a far stronger infrastructure than can be found in any alternative setting, thus shoring up prospects for sustainability.

Also, we saw that palliative care became the brand of the work rather than "end of life" even though there was a growing social movement to advocate for dying well. As a part of our assessment, we learned of data showing that patients and families resisted services labeled as providing hospice or end-of-life care, and we came to understand the reason for a shift in strategy and emphasis away from these terms to "palliative care." We have found that these linkages can only occur in conversation with the strategist(s).

From Retrospective to Prospective Evaluation

The three case studies in this volume of strategic evaluations are retrospective case studies. They were evaluations conducted by looking backwards. The IDRC evaluation featured in Chapter 2 was conducted to prepare the ground for a new strategic planning exercise. The RWJF End-of-Life evaluation featured in Chapter 3 began as a review of 10 years of grant making, and only became strategic when strategy became the theme that integrated the review. The Kellogg Devolution case in Chapter 4 applies a strategic lens retrospectively on a major U.S. federal government reform that became the focus of evaluation strategically. In this final section, we offer some thoughts about evaluating strategy *prospectively,* that is, when the evaluation is designed at the beginning of a strategic initiative.

For all strategy evaluations, the challenge is to assess merit and value within a strategic context. In the end-of-life study used as the methods example in this chapter, we had the advantage of a historical perspective. Focusing on outcomes (when we knew where to look for them) enabled us to reconstruct context to allow judgments regarding the strategy's merit. The retrospective nature of our assessment provided enormous grounding that could link specific outcomes to the strategy as we ultimately came to understand it.

Prospective evaluations need a different base to guide and determine relative merit and value. In essence, the evaluator needs to get into the minds of strategists to understand not just what they do, but how they learn and the instances where they have learned the most in the past. Understanding their triggers of insight can reveal the complex ways by which they make meaning of the world. This can inform a strategic evaluation design going forward, especially one focused on learning.

Beginning With Evaluation Criteria

The classic traditional evaluation approach to any evaluand, like evaluating *strategy,* is to identify criteria of excellence and then operationalize those

Table 5.1. Diverse Criteria for Evaluating Strategy

Characteristics of a strategy:
- Clear
- Explicit
- Attainable
- Communicable
- Meaningful
- Evaluatable/testable
- Affordable
- Attractive/magnetic/inspiring
- Research based/knowledge based

Criteria for evaluating relationships among elements of strategy:
- Coherence among different strategy elements
- Coherence between perspective and position
- Attention to and assistance with managing tensions between and among strategy dimensions
- Complexity of interrelationships
- Understanding of interdependence and interrelationships
- Evidence of systems thinking and complexity understandings

Characteristics of the organization's approach to strategy:
- Evidence of thoughtfulness in developing strategy
- Rigor of strategic planning
- Organization's commitment to being strategic (buy-in)
- Support for thinking strategically
- Norms and behaviors regarding the focus on strategy
- Alignment with mission
- Adaptability to changed conditions (environmental scanning and flexibility)
- Evidence of baseline for tracking strategy over time
- Commitment to evaluating strategy

Criteria for evaluating strategy execution:
- Linkage between decisions taken and overall strategic direction
- Evidence of learning
- Resources allocated on the basis of strategy
- Personnel decisions informed by strategy
- Commitment to evaluating strategy

criteria. In considering prospective evaluation of strategy, we undertook this exercise with philanthropic leaders, program officers, and evaluators at the Evaluation Roundtable. Table 5.1 shows the criteria for evaluating strategy that the group generated. This formed the basis for a lively discussion about criteria for evaluating strategy, the need for criteria to be appropriate to the context and values within which a particular evaluation of strategy unfolds, and limitations on the evaluation approach of focusing narrowly on singular and differentiated criteria.

However, assessing the overall quality of strategy requires a great deal more than the operationalization of distinct criteria such as coherence, alignment, and clarity. Although these characteristics may reveal inputs to strategy, they do not indicate whether the strategy is appropriate in varied contexts of interest or in response to numerous environmental challenges. Strategies that are coherent and aligned are not necessarily feasible, sellable, or effective. And the reverse is also true—the messiness of a body of work may reflect the need to test or adapt to a complex environment or to learn from failure. Thus, working with stakeholders to identify criteria for evaluating strategy can be a useful exercise to generate discussion about alternative criteria, but our experience suggests that it is important to look at the relationship among criteria and to be ever sensitive to the context within which those criteria were generated and to changes in the priorities given to various strategic criteria over time.

It is reasonable to expect coherence and alignment, but only in strategies that have evolved over time, reflecting maturity and learning. Standards of coherence and alignment (along with other criteria such as appropriate, evidence based, and so on) can be applied, but they should be considered in terms of context and capacity and balanced against performance and learning over time.

Strategy as Place Where Theory and Practice Intersect

If there is anything that we take away from this work it is that there is no "it" to strategy; strategy lives and changes all the time, whether this is acknowledged or not. In essence, the enterprise of strategy assessment is one of "sense making" (Weick, 1995).

We have come to see strategy as place where theory and practice intersect (or collide, as the case may be). A strategy assessment offers a prime opportunity to bring information to thinking and decision making such that reflection can occur. The evaluator can serve as a productive oppositional force to challenge assumptions—with data—and help the strategist examine and if need be revise hypotheses as they play out in real contexts. Quoting Mintzberg at the Evaluation Roundtable, "strategy is learned and not planned."

Further, if we cast strategy evaluation at the intersection of thought and action (Mintzberg, Ahlstrand, & Lampel, 1998), the evaluator can enter into a relationship with the strategist as a reflective practitioner (Schon, 1995) and take advantage of what Schon has called "tacit knowing in action." This is the ability of competent practitioners (our strategists) to identify, name, and put together phenomena in a way associated with their knowledge, training, and experience such that it becomes second nature. Like jazz musicians who feel their way into their material, so, too, do those who construct and enact strategy. And so, too, must those who evaluate strategy, if they are to be in tune with the strategists and executors of strategy who are adapting as they learn. Developmental evaluation (Patton, 2010) is especially appropriate in this regard because it specifically engages innovators in adapting to the emergent realities of what unfolds as strategy and vision are

Table 5.2. Generic Evaluation Framework for Tracking Strategies: Key Questions

Beginning Point: Strategic Baseline	Tracking Along the Way	At Some Designated End Point: Strategic Review
What is the strategic intent?	What aspects of the strategy are fully implemented? What factors contributed to realization?	What of what was intended was accomplished?
If the strategy is successful, what will have occurred?	What aspects of the strategy are unrealized, are left behind, or are abandoned? Why?	What was learned about those dimensions of the strategy that were not realized?
What are the expected and hoped-for results of the strategy?	What new opportunities emerged that were incorporated into or altered the strategic direction?	What was accomplished from what emerged along the way? How did these emergent elements affect overall strategic direction and realization?

translated into actions. Developmental evaluation provides a prospective framework for tracking strategies that anticipates that some aspects of strategy will be implemented as envisioned, some aspects of strategy will not be realized, and some unanticipated opportunities will emerge that will be incorporated into and thereby alter what takes place at the intersection between strategic intent and strategy execution. Table 5.2 highlights these strategic evaluation questions.

The message from this is that strategy assessment is inextricably a partnership between strategist and evaluator and cannot be productively disassociated from the doing. Therefore, this is not work for those who seek distance and objectivity. At its heart, strategy evaluation is an enterprise of serious and critical appreciation.

What Is the Yield?

There is a cost and benefit to strategy evaluations. They require time, resources, a commitment to data collection, and a relationship with the strategist in a process of learning about their work. A mentor once called it the "shared work of worry." But the yield can be sizeable. Our experience applying this method has offered the following benefits:

Identifying gaps in program, or missing elements of action or actors.
Understanding context, environmental forces, and responses.

Understanding reactions of people and institutions.

Pinpointing patterns in implementation problems.

Surfacing testable hypotheses and revising them.

Learning from specific ventures and knowing when to persist and when to withdraw or expand efforts.

Spotting tensions between and among varying perspectives.

Recognizing tensions between perspective and position.

Improving understanding of relevant actors and their roles and relationships.

And, ultimately, taking strides in learning, strategy evolution, and execution.

References

Field, M., & Cassel, C.K. (Eds.). (1997.) *Approaching death, improving care at the end of life*. Washington, DC: Committee on Care at the End of Life, Division of Health Care Services, Institute of Medicine. National Academies Press.

Guth, R. A. (2010, April 23). Gates rethinks his war on polio. *Wall Street Journal*. Retrieved from http://online.wsj.com/article/SB10001424052702303348504575184093239615022.html?KEYWORDS=Gates+Rethinks+His+War+on+Polio

Mintzberg, H. (1994). *The rise and fall of strategic planning: Reconceiving roles for planning, plans, planners*. New York: The Free Press.

Mintzberg, H. (2007). *Tracking strategies, toward a general theory of strategy formation*. Oxford: Oxford University Press.

Mintzberg, H., Ahlstrand, B., & Lampel, J. (1998). *Strategy safari: A guided tour through the wilds of strategic management*. New York: The Free Press.

Patrizi, P. A. (2010). *Use of evaluative information in foundations: Benchmarking data*. Philadelphia: Patrizi Associates.

Patton, M. Q. (2010). *Developmental evaluation: Applying complexity concepts to enhance innovation and use*. New York: Guilford Press.

Schon, D. (1995). *The reflective practitioner: How professsionals think in action*. New York: Basic Books.

Weick, K. (1995). *Sensemaking in organizations*. Thousand Oaks, CA: Sage.

Weisfeld, V., Miller, D., Gibson, R., & Schroeder, S. (2000, November/December). Improving care at the end of life: What does it take? *Health Affairs*, pp. 277–283.

PATRICIA A. PATRIZI *is chair of the Evaluation Roundtable and principal of Patrizi Associates, Philadelphia.*

INDEX